First Edition

I0176823

Taste of Transcendence

Sacred Scripture, Stories, & Teachings from the World's Religious Traditions

Javy W Galindo

Enlightened Hyena Press
Los Altos, CA
www.HyenaPress.com

This book is published by Enlightened Hyena Press.
2310 Homestead Rd, C1 #125
Los Altos, CA
www.HyenaPress.com

Printed and bound in the United States of America.

Although the author and publisher have made every effort to ensure the accuracy and completeness of information contained in this book, we assume no responsibility for errors, inaccuracies, omissions, or any inconsistency herein. Any slights on people, places, or organizations are unintentional.

First Paperback Edition
ISBN 978-1-7345631-0-8

Book Design: EH Designs

ATTENTION CORPORATIONS, UNIVERSITIES, COLLEGES, PROFESSIONAL, ORGANIZATIONS— DISCOUNT ON BULK PURCHASES AVAILABLE.

For information, please contact the publisher:
www.HyenaPress.com, info@hyenapress.com, (408) 819-3715

Table of Contents

INTRODUCTION

"The study of religion, like the study of poetry, brings us face to face with the fundamental principles of human nature. Religion, whether it be natural religion or that which is formulated in a book, is as universal as poetry, and like poetry, existed before letters and writing. It is only in a serious and sympathetic frame of mind that we should approach the rudest forms of these two departments of human activity."

Epiphanius Wilson,
author of *Sacred Books of the East*.

Source: *Sacred Books of the East*. Oxford University Press, 1900.

What is a Religion?

The word "religion" has roots in the Latin term that refers to things that bind. In many ways, what we often think of as being religious are those customs, beliefs, rituals, practices, art, architecture, texts, teachings, songs, stories, and other artifacts that we use to keep us together. They are things that bind us to one another and keep us from personally falling apart in the face of the inherent adversities of life.

In modern times, religion is often associated with certain peoples who have a belief in the existence of a transcendent reality. This transcendent reality has been called many things: Brahman, Nirvana, the Tao, YHWH, Lord, Christ, God, Heaven, the Great Spirit, and many more. The post-enlightenment mind has had a preoccupation with knowing whether or not these transcendent realities exist. The ancient Greeks referred to this type of knowledge as *logos*. Logos refers to knowledge that provides a rational account of the world. "Does the Tao actually exist? Was Jesus really resurrected from the dead?" Logos is knowledge of facts; of whether a statement is true or false.

However, the ancient Greeks also acknowledged the existence of another type of knowledge that is beyond being true or false. They referred to this type of knowledge as *mythos*. This is the knowledge of experience, meaning, and familiarity. To say that you know anger, fear, or love is to say you have experienced it. When one says they know your mother, they are not necessarily saying they possess facts about your mother. They are saying they are familiar with her, that they have met her and shared experiences with her. This type of knowledge is difficult to convey with declarative statements of fact. No matter how much I try to explain to you rationally what my mother means to me, you will never really know what she means to me from my statements of facts. However, you may get a sense through the stories I tell of her (regardless of accuracy) or through the songs I sing when I think about her, because both are meant to invoke an experience.

This book aims to provide mythos knowledge of the world's religious traditions.

Within these pages are the teachings, scriptures, stories, and songs that have given people an experience of a transcendent reality. To say it differently, they refer to a life beyond the one these people had been conditioned to experience. They point to a way of experiencing the world that transcends the typical veil of culture to see what is ultimately possible for a human life.

In other words, beyond normal human vices, beyond impulsive responses to fear and hardship, and beyond popular culture's perspectives on how your life should be lived, these traditions say there lies something more wonderous, meaningful, valuable, and real.

Hence, this is a book about religion in the most basic sense of the term. In this book are words that have been used to bind people together through their ability to express an experience of a transcendent life.

Part I:
Vedic Traditions

CHAPTER ONE
Hinduism

To the Unknown God
(A hymn from the *Vedas*)

***

In the beginning there arose the Golden Child. As soon as born, he alone was the lord of all that is. He established the earth and this heaven:—Who is the God to whom we shall offer sacrifice?

He who gives breath, he who gives strength, whose command all the bright gods revere, whose shadow is immortality, whose shadow is death:—Who is the God to whom we shall offer sacrifice?

He who through his might became the sole king of the breathing and twinkling world, who governs all this, man and beast:—Who is the God to whom we shall offer sacrifice?

He through whose might these snowy mountains are, and the sea, they say, with the distant river; he of whom these regions are indeed the two arms:—Who is the God to whom we shall offer sacrifice?

He through whom the awful heaven and the earth were made fast, he through whom the ether was established, and the firmament; he who measured the air in the sky:—Who is the God to whom we shall offer sacrifice?

He to whom heaven and earth, standing firm by his will, look up, trembling in their mind, he over whom the risen sun shines forth:—Who is the God to whom we shall offer sacrifice?

When the great waters went everywhere, holding the germ, and

Source: from a translation by Max Muller found in *Sacred Books of the East*. Oxford University Press, 1900.

generating light, then there arose from them the breath of the gods:—Who is the God to whom we shall offer sacrifice?

He who by his might looked even over the waters which held power and generated the sacrifice, he who alone is God above all gods:—Who is the God to whom we shall offer sacrifice?

May he not hurt us, he who is the begetter of the earth, or he, the righteous, who begat the heaven; he who also begat the bright and mighty waters:—Who is the God to whom we shall offer sacrifice?

Pragâpati, no other than thou embraces all these created things. May that be ours which we desire when sacrificing to thee: may we be lords of wealth!

Brahman: The Ground of all Being

(Excerpts from the *Isra Upanishads*)

***

Ultimate Reality

OM! That Invisible Absolute (Brahman) is whole;
Whole is the visible universe;
From Brahman comes forth the universe.
Though the universe has come out from Brahman,
Yet Brahman remains unaltered and perfect.
OM! Herein lies peace! Peace! Peace!

The True Self

All this, whatsoever exists in the universe, is full of the Lord.
Having renounced maya, enjoy Brahman. Do not covet the
wealth of any man.

If one should desire to live in this world a hundred years,
one should live performing Karma (righteous deeds). Thus thou
mayest live; there is no other way. By doing this, Karma (the
fruits of thy actions) will not defile thee.

After leaving their bodies, they who have rejected the true
Self (Atman) go to the worlds of the Asuras (demons), covered
with blinding ignorance.

The Self, though motionless, is swifter than the mind. The
senses can never overtake It, for It ever goes before. Though
immovable, the Self travels faster than those who run. It sustains
all living beings.

The Self moves and It moves not. It is far and also It is near.
It is within and also It is without all this.

He who sees all beings in the Self and the Self in all beings,

Source: *The Upanishads,* translated by Swami Paramananda, 1919.

he never turns away from It.

He who perceives all beings as the Self for him how can there be delusion or grief, when he sees this oneness (everywhere)?

Brahman is all-encircling, resplendent, bodiless, spotless, without sinews, pure, untouched by sin, all-seeing, all-knowing, transcendent, self-existent; this true Self has disposed all things duly for eternal years.

Escaping the Wheel of Samsara

(Excerpts from the *Katha Upanishads*)

***

There are two who enjoy the fruits of their good deeds in the world, having entered into the cave of the heart, seated (there) on the highest summit...

...Know the Atman (Self) as the lord of the chariot, and the body as the chariot. Know also the intellect to be the driver and mind the reins.

The senses are called the horses; the sense objects are the roads; when the Atman is united with body, senses and mind, then the wise call Him the enjoyer.

He who is without discrimination and whose mind is always uncontrolled, his senses are unmanageable, like the vicious horses of a driver.

But he who is full of discrimination and whose mind is always controlled, his senses are manageable, like the good horses of a driver.

He who does not possess discrimination, whose mind is uncontrolled and always impure, he does not reach that goal, but falls again into Samsara (realm of birth and death).

But he who possesses right discrimination, whose mind is under control and always pure, he reaches that goal, from which he is not born again.

The man who has a discriminative intellect for the driver, and a controlled mind for the reins, reaches the end of the journey, the highest place of Vishnu (the All-pervading and Unchangeable One).

Beyond the senses are the objects, beyond the objects is the mind, beyond the mind is the intellect, beyond the intellect is the great Atman.

Beyond the great Atman is the Unmanifested; beyond the

Source: *The Upanishads,* translated by Swami Paramananda, 1919.

Unmanifested is the Purusha (the Cosmic Soul); beyond the Purusha there is nothing. That is the end, that is the final goal.

This Atman (Self), hidden in all beings, does not shine forth; but It is seen by subtle seers through keen and subtle understanding.

A wise man should control speech by mind, mind by intellect, intellect by the great Atman, and that by the Peaceful One (the true Self)

The Path of Knowledge
(Excerpts from *The Bhagavad-Gita*)

The Bhagavad Gita ("Song of Celestials") is the sixth section of the poetic epic entitled Mahabarata. This poetic epic tells the tale of a long and difficult war. The Bhagavad Gita deals specifically with a warrior-prince named Arjuna who looks at his enemies on the battlefield and recognizes them: they are his friends and family. He is distraught and does not know whether he should do his warrior duty and fight or lay down his weapon. In the excerpt below, he begins to ask advice from his charioteer, Krishna, who is the avatar of the god Vishnu.

***

Sanjaya (narrator).
Him, filled with such compassion and such grief,
With eyes tear-dimmed, despondent, in stern words
The charioteer, thus addressed:

Krishna.
How hath this weakness taken thee? Whence springs
The inglorious trouble, shameful to the brave,
Barring the path of virtue? Nay, Arjun!
Forbid thyself to feebleness! it mars
Thy warrior-name! cast off the coward-fit!
Wake! Be thyself! Arise, Scourge of thy Foes!

Arjuna.
How can I, in the battle, shoot with shafts
On Bhishma, or on Drona-O thou Chief!--
Both worshipful, both honourable men?

Source: *The Bhagavad-Gita*, translated by Sir Edwin Arnold. Truslove, Hanson & Comba, Ltd, 1900.

23

Better to live on beggar's bread
With those we love alive,
Than taste their blood in rich feasts spread,
And guiltily survive!
Ah! were it worse-who knows?--to be
Victor or vanquished here,
When those confront us angrily
Whose death leaves living drear?
In pity lost, by doubtings tossed,
My thoughts-distracted-turn
To Thee, the Guide I reverence most,
That I may counsel learn:
I know not what would heal the grief
Burned into soul and sense,
If I were left standing—the king
But all whom I loved were gone.

Sanjaya.
So spake Arjuna to the Lord of Hearts,
And sighing "I will not fight!" held silence then.
To whom, with tender smile,
While the Prince wept despairing the battle
Krishna made answer in divinest verse:

Krishna.
Thou grievest where no grief should be! thou speak'st
Words lacking wisdom! for the wise in heart
Mourn not for those that live, nor those that die.
Nor I, nor thou, nor any one of these,
We have never not existed,
Nor will we ever cease to exist.
All, that doth live, lives always! To man's frame
As there come infancy and youth and age,
So come there raisings-up and layings-down
Of other and of other life-abodes,
Which the wise know, and fear not. This that irks--

Thy sense-life, thrilling to the elements--
Bringing thee heat and cold, sorrows and joys,
'Tis brief and mutable! Bear with it, Prince!
As the wise bear. The true Self which is not moved,
The Self that with a strong and constant calm
Takes sorrow and takes joy indifferently,
Lives in the life undying! That which is
Can never cease to be; that which is not
Will not exist. To see this truth of both
Is theirs who part essence from accident,
Substance from shadow. Indestructible,
Learn thou! the Life is, spreading life through all;
It cannot anywhere, by any means,
Be anywise diminished, stayed, or changed.
But for these fleeting frames which it informs
With spirit deathless, endless, infinite,
They perish. Let them perish, Prince! and fight!
He who shall say, "Lo! I have slain a man!"
He who shall think, "Lo! I am slain!" those both
Know naught! Life cannot slay. Life is not slain!
Never the spirit was born; the spirit shall cease to be never;
Never was time it was not;
End and Beginning are dreams!
Birthless and deathless and changeless
remaineth the spirit forever;
Death hath not touched it at all,
dead though the house of it seems!

Who knoweth it exhaustless, self-sustained,
Immortal, indestructible, --shall such
Say, "I have killed a man, or caused to kill?"

Nay, but as when one layeth
His worn-out robes away,
And taking new ones, sayeth,
"These will I wear to-day!"

So putteth by the spirit
Lightly its garb of flesh,
And passeth to inherit
A residence afresh.

I say to thee weapons reach not the Life;
Flame burns it not, waters cannot o'erwhelm,
Nor dry winds wither it. Impenetrable,
Unentered, unassailed, unharmed, untouched,
Immortal, all-arriving, stable, sure,
Invisible, ineffable, by word
And thought uncompassed, ever all itself,
Thus is the Soul declared! How wilt thou, then,--
Knowing it so,--grieve when thou shouldst not grieve?
How, if thou hearest that the man new-dead
Is, like the man new-born, still living man--
One same, existent Brahman--wilt thou weep?
The end of birth is death; the end of death
Is birth: this is ordained! and mournest thou,
Chief of the stalwart arm! for what befalls
Which could not otherwise befall? The birth
Of living things comes unperceived; the death
Comes unperceived; between them, beings perceive:
What is there sorrowful herein, dear Prince?

Wonderful, wistful, to contemplate!
Difficult, doubtful, to speak upon!
Strange and great for tongue to relate,
Mystical hearing for everyone!
Nor wotteth man this, what a marvel it is,
When seeing, and saying, and hearing are done!

This Life within all living things, my Prince!
Hides beyond harm; scorn thou to suffer, then,
For that which cannot suffer. Do thy duty!
Be mindful of thy name, and tremble not!

Naught better can betide a martial soul
Than lawful war; happy the warrior
To whom comes joy of battle--comes, as now,
Glorious and fair, unsought; opening for him
A gateway unto Heav'n. But, if thou shunn'st
This honourable field--
If, knowing thy duty and thy task, thou bidd'st
Duty and task go by--that shall be sin!

And those to come shall speak thee infamy
From age to age; but infamy is worse
For men of noble blood to bear than death!
The chiefs upon their battle-chariots
Will deem 'twas fear that drove thee from the fray.
Of those who held thee mighty-souled the scorn
Thou must abide, while all thine enemies
Will scatter bitter speech of thee, to mock
The valour which thou hadst; what fate could fall
More grievously than this? Either--being killed--
Thou wilt win safety, or--alive
And victor--thou wilt reign an earthly king.
Therefore, arise! brace
Thine arm for conflict, nerve thy heart to meet--
As things alike to thee--pleasure or pain,
Profit or ruin, victory or defeat:
So minded, gird thee to the fight, for so
Thou shalt not sin!
Thus far I speak to thee
As from unspiritually--

Hear now the deeper teaching of the jnana
Which holding, understanding, thou shalt burst
The bondage of wrought deeds.
Here shall no end be hindered, no hope marred,
No loss be feared: faith--yea, a little faith--
Shall save thee from the anguish of thy dread.

Here shines one rule--
One steadfast rule--while shifting souls have laws
Many and hard. Specious, but wrongful deem
The speech of those ill-taught ones who extol
The letter of their Vedas, saying, "This
Is all we have, or need;" being weak at heart
With wants, seekers of ananda (bliss): which comes--they say--
From the law of karma, promising men
Much profit in new births for works of faith;
Through many rituals and acts
One shall accrue towards wealth and power;
But they stay trapped in the wheel of samsara.

On heavenly meditation, much these teach,
From Vedas, concerning the "three qualities;"
But thou, be free of the "three qualities,"
(1) Free of the "pairs of opposites,"
(2) free from judgmental thoughts, and
(3) free from the desire for materialistic abundance.
Look! like as when a tank pours water forth
To suit all needs, so do the true seekers draw
Text for all wants from tank of the Vedas.

But thou, want not! ask not! Find full reward
Of doing right in right! Let right deeds be
Thy motive, not the fruit which comes from them.
And live in action! Labour! Make thine acts
Thy piety, casting all self aside,
Contemning gain and merit; equable
In good or evil: equability
This is jnana. Is true karma yoga!

Yet, the right act
Is less, far less, than the right-thinking mind.
Seek refuge in thy soul; have there moksha (liberation)!
Scorn them that follow virtue for her gifts!

The mind of pure devotion--even here--
Casts equally aside good deeds and bad,
Passing above them. Unto pure devotion
Devote thyself: with perfect meditation
Comes karma (perfect act), and the right-hearted rise--
More certainly because of karma yoga (they seek no gain)--
Forth from the bands of body, step by step,
To highest seats of ananda (bliss). When thy firm soul
Hath shaken off those tangled oracles
Which ignorantly guide, then shall it soar
To high neglect of what's denied or said,
This way or that way, in doctrinal writ.
Troubled no longer by the priestly lore,
Safe shall it live, and sure; steadfastly bent
On meditation. This is jnana--and Peace!

Arjuna.
What is the mark of moksha;
Of a man who has reunited with Brahman?
Confirmed in holy meditation? How
Know we his speech? Sits he, moves he
Like other men?

Krishna.
When one
Abandoning desires which shake the mind--
Finds in his soul full comfort for his soul,
He hath attained the jnana--that man is such!
In sorrows not dejected, and in joys
Not overjoyed; dwelling outside the stress
Of passion, fear, and anger; fixed in calms
Of lofty contemplation.
He who to none and nowhere overbound
By ties of flesh, takes evil things and good
Neither desponding nor exulting, such
Bears wisdom's plainest mark! He who shall draw

As the wise tortoise draws its four feet safe
Under its shield, his five frail senses back
Under the spirit's buckler from the world
Which else assails them, such a one, my Prince!
Hath wisdom's mark! Things that solicit sense
Hold off from the self-governed; nay, it comes,
The appetites of him who lives beyond
Depart,--aroused no more. Yet may it chance,
O Son of Kunti! that a governed mind
Shall some time feel the sense-storms sweep, and wrest
Strong self-control by the roots. Let him regain
His kingdom! let him conquer this, and sit
On Me intent. That man alone is wise
Who keeps the mastery of himself! If one
Ponders on objects of the sense, there springs
Attraction; from attraction grows desire,
Desire flames to fierce passion, passion breeds
Recklessness; then the memory--all betrayed--
Lets noble purpose go, and saps the mind,
Till purpose, mind, and man are all undone.
But, if one deals with objects of the sense
Not loving and not hating, making them
Serve his free soul, which rests serenely lord,
Lo! such a man comes to tranquility;
And out of that tranquility shall rise
The end and healing of his earthly pains,
Since the will governed sets the soul at peace.
The soul of the ungoverned is not his,
Nor hath he knowledge of himself; which lacked,
How grows serenity? and, wanting that,
Whence shall he hope for happiness?

The mind
That gives itself to follow shows of sense
Seeth its helm of wisdom rent away,
And, like a ship in waves of whirlwind, drives

To wreck and death. Only with him, great Prince!
Whose senses are not swayed by things of sense--
Only with him who holds his mastery,
Shows wisdom perfect. What is midnight-gloom
To unenlightened souls shines wakeful day
To his clear gaze; what seems as wakeful day
Is known for night, thick night of ignorance,
To his true-seeing eyes. Such is the Saint!

And like the ocean, day by day receiving
Floods from all lands, which never overflows
Its boundary-line not leaping, and not leaving,
Fed by the rivers, but never disturbed.

So is the perfect one! to his soul's ocean
The world of sense pours streams of maya (illusion);
But these streams, cannot disturb him,
Cannot upend the calmness of his inner sea.

Yea! whoso, shaking off the yoke of flesh
Lives lord, not servant, of his lusts; set free
From pride, from passion, from the sin of maya;
Toucheth tranquillity! O Pritha's Son!
That is the state of moksha! There rests no dread
When that last step is reached! Live where he will,
Die when he may,
He and Brahman are one.

CHAPTER TWO
Buddhism

The Origin of the Buddha

***

The Prophesy

There once lived an Indian prince named Siddhartha. His mother and father were rulers of a wealthy kingdom. Upon his birth, a spirit visited the king and queen with a message about their child:

"My king, your son is to have one of two paths in life. The first: he is to be a great ruler of your kingdom, bringing great wealth and treasures to your land. The second: he is to be the great redeemer of the world but live as a popper."

The mother and father were aghast at this news and did not want their son to live as a popper. They asked the spirit what could be done to ensure their son becomes a great ruler.

"You must ensure that he never leaves your kingdom," replied the spirit.

At that, the king and queen devised a plan. "We will ensure that his every need is met. We will ensure that his every desire is fulfilled. He will be adored by all in the kingdom and never have to experience worry or regret."

As the years went by, the king and queen followed their plan. The infant prince received constant affection, attention, and adoration. The boy prince received all the toys and trinkets he could ever want, and extravagant food and drink were never in short supply. The teenage prince enjoyed festivities and relations with the most beautiful women in the kingdom.

And throughout it all, his parents never allowed a sight to enter their palace that would disturb his mind and make him worry or regret.

Once the prince became a young man, his father was eager to have him married. "Surely this will keep my son bound to our kingdom," thought the elderly king. And soon the prince married

---

Source: original adaptation by the author.

and had his own son.

The Four Sights

Prince Siddhartha was soon to be King Siddhartha. But he thought to himself, *what kind of king has never ventured beyond his own palace walls and not known his own kingdom? I have received all that I have ever desired and to know my kingdom is what I now desire.*

With his personal guard as his only companion, the prince took his first steps outside of his palace walls and had his first intimate sights of the kingdom.

His first sight was that of a wrinkled man, hair of white, stooped over a stick, struggling to walk and stand. "What is this?" asked the prince.

"Old age," replied his companion. "It comes to us all."

Comes to us all? The prince was aghast at this reality.

His second sight was that of a woman coughing uncontrollably, wincing, and writhing in pain. "What is this?" asked the prince.

"This is illness," replied his companion. "It comes to us all."

Comes to us all? The prince was again aghast at this reality.

His third sight was that of a body, limp, unmoving, carried away by others. "What do I see here?" asked the prince.

"This is death," replied his companion. "It is a permanent sleep. This too comes to us all no matter how much we might try to escape it."

The prince was in horror.

Finally, he saw the sight of a beggar, dressed in rags, humbly asking for food, but without shame or distress. "Is this inevitable too?" asked the prince.

"No," replied his companion. "This is an ascetic. One who has renounced worldly pleasures in search of a higher truth."

The prince then returned to his palace, distraught over all the suffering he had seen upon his first real view of the kingdom. *Life makes us old, ill, and eventually takes away our life, itself. So much suffering...*

That night he could not sleep, his mind full of worry and regret. He gazed longingly at his wife and newborn child and his thoughts wandered to what life would eventually make of them. He then looked out his window and his thoughts wandered to what life would eventually make of all his people. He then imagined all the people of the world and his thoughts wandered to what life would make of all of them.

I have always received what I have desired, and now what I desire is to end this suffering.

That night the prince grieved, for he knew that he had to leave behind his parents, his wife, his infant son, and all the wealth and pleasures of the kingdom to venture out in search of a solution to this suffering.

Searching for Suffering's Solution

Early the next morning, with a gentle kiss to his beloveds while they slept, he left his princely life behind in search of a solution to suffering.

He first went out and lived the life of a beggar, hoping that a life of humility would lead him to a solution. After some time striving for a humble life, he failed to find a solution to suffering.

He then searched for spiritual teachers who taught him many religious practices, meditation techniques, and beliefs they claimed stemmed from the wisest gurus and the most sacred scriptures. After some time striving for a spiritual life, he failed to find a solution to suffering.

He then found a group of devotees who taught the ways of asceticism. "You must renounce not just material wants and desires," stated the devotees. "But to attain true liberation, you must renounce all bodily wants and desires." The prince was determined to dedicate himself to this practice. He soon became the most skilled devotee, outlasting all others when it came to fasting and living without the warmth of a fire on the coldest days. He even struck himself with weeds and vines, causing himself harm so he could practice overcoming pain. After some time striving for an ascetic life, he became weak and frail, and still he failed to find a solution to suffering.

The Temptation

He wanted so badly to end suffering. He tried so hard to find a solution. What was left for him to try? What was left for him to do? Siddhartha soon decided that it was time to simply sit, rest, and stop his striving. Instead of trying to find the solution to suffering, he thought his final course of action was to be patient and allow the solution to find him.

It was now entering the warmer months, so the former prince found a large, sturdy fig tree, and began to meditate within its shade, determined to wait patiently for a solution to suffering. Days upon days came and went. Siddhartha continued to sit and meditate with focused attention and intention. The evil spirit Māra was determined to stop Siddhartha. For to find a way to extinguish suffering was to also find a way to extinguish Māra. So, the evil spirit would try all he could to distract the Siddhartha and cloud his mind so a solution would not be seen. Māra attempted to distract him with thoughts of wealth, women, wine and the most delicious delicacies the world could offer. However, no matter how hard Māra tried, he was unsuccessful at disturbing the former prince. Siddhartha continued to sit and meditate with focused attention and intention.

Siddhartha Becomes the Buddha

Then on the seventh night of his seventh week under the fig tree, he finally awoke from his meditation.

"I now see that reality has three marks. First, life is dukkha (suffering). Second, life is anicca (ever-changing). And third, life is anatta (no self exists in reality)."

And from these observations of existence, he determined the nature of suffering, the cause of suffering, the nature of non-suffering, and the means of escaping suffering. These he deemed the Four Noble Truths.

And from this point forward, Siddhartha had transformed into a Buddha, the enlightened (awoken) one.

The Four Noble Truths

(Excerpts from *Jātaka Tales*)

***

The Bodhisattva (one on the path to enlightenment), having put Māra (the deceiver) to flight, gave himself up to meditation. All the miseries of the world, the evils produced by evil deeds and the sufferings arising therefrom, passed before his mental eye, and he thought:

"Surely if living creatures saw the results of all their evil deeds, they would turn away from them in disgust. But selfhood blinds them, and they cling to their obnoxious desires.

"They crave pleasure for themselves and they cause pain to others; when death destroys their individuality, they find no peace; their thirst for existence abides and their selfhood reappears in new births.

"Thus, they continue to move in the coil and can find no escape from the hell of their own making. And how empty are their pleasures, how vain are their endeavors! Hollow like the plantain-tree and without contents like the bubble.

"The world is full of evil and sorrow, because it is full of lust. Men go astray because they think that delusion is better than truth. Rather than truth they follow error, which is pleasant to look at in the beginning but in the end causes anxiety, tribulation, and misery."

And the Bodhisattva began to expound the Dharma (teachings). The Dharma is the truth. The Dharma is the sacred law. The Dharma is religion. The Dharma alone can deliver us from error, from wrong and from sorrow.

Pondering on the origin of birth and death, the Enlightened One recognized that ignorance was the root of all evil; and these are the links in the development of life, called the twelve nidānas:

Source: *The Gospel of the Buddha,* compiled by Paul Carus. The Open Court Publishing Company, 1915.

In the beginning there is existence blind and without knowledge; and in this sea of ignorance there are stirrings formative and organizing. From stirrings, formative and organizing, rises awareness or feelings. Feelings beget organisms that live as individual beings. These organisms develop the six fields, that is, the five senses and the mind. The six fields come in contact with things. Contact begets sensation. Sensation creates the thirst of individualized being. The thirst of being creates a cleaving to things. The cleaving produces the growth and continuation of selfhood. Selfhood continues in renewed births. The renewed births of selfhood are the cause of suffering, old age, sickness, and death. They produce lamentation, anxiety, and despair.

The cause of all sorrow lies at the very beginning; it is hidden in the ignorance from which life grows. Remove ignorance and you will destroy the wrong appetences that rise from ignorance; destroy these appetences and you will wipe out the wrong perception that rises from them. Destroy wrong perception and there is an end of errors in individualized beings. Destroy the errors in individualized beings and the illusions of the six fields will disappear. Destroy illusions and the contact with things will cease to beget misconception. Destroy misconception and you do away with thirst. Destroy thirst and you will be free of ail morbid cleaving. Remove the cleaving and you destroy the selfishness of selfhood. If the selfishness of selfhood is destroyed you will be above birth, old age, disease, and death, and you will escape all suffering.

The Enlightened One saw the four noble truths which point out the path that leads to Nirvana or the extinction of self:

The first noble truth is the existence of sorrow.

The second noble truth is the cause of suffering.

The third noble truth is the cessation of sorrow.

The fourth noble truth is the eightfold path that leads to the cessation of sorrow.

This is the Dharma. This is the truth. This is religion. And the Enlightened One uttered this stanza:

"Through many births I sought in vain
The Builder of this House of Pain.
Now, Builder, thee I plainly see!
This is the last abode for me.
Thy gable's yoke and rafters broke,
My heart has peace. All lust will cease."

There is self and there is truth. Where self is, truth is not. Where truth is, self is not. Self is the fleeting error of samsāra; it is individual separateness and that egotism which begets envy and hatred. Self is the yearning for pleasure and the lust after vanity. Truth is the correct comprehension of things; it is the permanent and everlasting, the real in all existence, the bliss of righteousness.

The existence of self is an illusion, and there is no wrong in this world, no vice, no evil, except what flows from the assertion of self.

The attainment of truth is possible only when self is recognized as an illusion. Righteousness can be practiced only when we have freed our mind from passions of egotism. Perfect peace can dwell only where all vanity has disappeared.

Blessed is he who has understood the Dharma. Blessed is he who does no harm to his fellow-beings. Blessed is he who overcomes wrong and is free from passion. To the highest bliss has he attained who has conquered all selfishness and vanity. He has become the Buddha, the Perfect One, the Blessed One, the Holy One.

Samsara & No Self

(from *The Gospel of the Buddha*)

***

Look about and contemplate life! Everything is transient and nothing endures. There is birth and death, growth and decay; there is combination and separation.

The glory of the world is like a flower: it stands in full bloom in the morning and fades in the heat of the day.

Wherever you look, there is a rushing and a struggling, and an eager pursuit of pleasure. There is a panic flight from pain and death, and hot are the flames of burning desires. The world is vanity fair, full of changes and transformations. All is Samsāra.

Is there nothing permanent in the world? Is there in the universal turmoil no resting-place where our troubled heart can find peace? Is there nothing everlasting?

Oh, that we could have cessation of anxiety, that our burning desires would be extinguished! When shall the mind become tranquil and composed?

The Buddha (enlightened one), our Lord, was grieved at the ills of life. He saw the vanity of worldly happiness and sought salvation in the one thing that will not fade or perish, but will abide for ever and ever.

Ye who long for life, know that immortality is hidden in transiency. Ye who wish for happiness without the sting of regret, lead a life of righteousness. Ye who yearn for riches, receive treasures that are eternal. Truth is wealth, and a life of truth is happiness.

All compounds will be dissolved again, but the verities which determine all combinations and separations as laws of nature endure forever and aye. Bodies fall to dust, but the truths of the mind will not be destroyed.

Source: *The Gospel of the Buddha,* compiled by Paul Carus. The Open Court Publishing Company, 1915.

Truth knows neither birth nor death; it has no beginning and no end. Welcome the truth. The truth is the immortal part of mind.

Establish the truth in your mind, for the truth is the image of the eternal; it portrays the immutable; it reveals the everlasting; the truth gives unto mortals the boon of immortality.

The Buddha has proclaimed the truth; let the truth of the Buddha dwell in your hearts. Extinguish in yourselves every desire that antagonizes the Buddha, and in the perfection of your spiritual growth you will become like unto him.

That of your heart which cannot or will not develop into Buddha must perish, for it is mere illusion and unreal; it is the source of your error; it is the cause of your misery.

You attain to immortality by filling your minds with truth. Therefore, become like unto vessels fit to receive the Master's words. Cleanse yourselves of evil and sanctify your lives. There is no other way of reaching truth.

Learn to distinguish between Self and Truth. Self is the cause of selfishness and the source of evil; truth cleaves to no self; it is universal and leads to justice and righteousness.

Self, that which seems to those who love their self as their being, is not the eternal, the everlasting, the imperishable. Seek not self, but seek the truth.

If we liberate our souls from our petty selves, wish no ill to others, and become clear as a crystal diamond reflecting the light of truth, what a radiant picture will appear in us mirroring things as they are, without the admixture of burning desires, without the distortion of erroneous illusion, without the agitation of clinging and unrest.

Yet ye love self and will not abandon self-love. So be it, but then, verily, ye should learn to distinguish between the false self and the true self. The ego with all its egotism is the false self. It is an unreal illusion and a perishable combination. He only who identifies his self with the truth will attain Nirvana; and he who has entered Nirvana has attained Buddhahood; he has acquired the highest good; he has become eternal and immortal.

All compound things shall be dissolved again, worlds will break to pieces and our individualities will be scattered; but the words of the Buddha will remain forever.

The extinction of self is salvation; the annihilation of self is the condition of enlightenment; the blotting out of self is Nirvana. Happy is he who has ceased to live for pleasure and rests in the truth. Verily his composure and tranquility of mind are the highest bliss.

Let us take our refuge in the Buddha, for he has found the everlasting in the transient. Let us take our refuge in that which is the immutable in the changes of existence. Let us take our refuge in the truth that is established through the enlightenment of the Buddha. Let us take our refuge in the community of those who seek the truth and endeavor to live in the truth.

The Way of Truth
(Excerpts from *The Dhammapada*)

***

The Pairs

All that we are is the result of what we have thought: it is founded on our thoughts; it is made up of our thoughts. If a man speaks or acts with an evil thought, pain follows him, as the wheel follows the foot of the ox that draws the carriage.

All that we are is the result of what we have thought: it is founded on our thoughts; it is made up of our thoughts. If a man speaks or acts with a pure thought, happiness follows him, like a shadow that never leaves him.

"He abused me, he beat me, he defeated me, he robbed me"— in those who harbor such thoughts hatred will never cease.

"He abused me, he beat me, he defeated me, he robbed me"— in those who do not harbor such thoughts hatred will cease.

For hatred does not cease by hatred at any time: hatred ceases by love—this is an old rule.

The world does not know that we must all come to an end here; but those who know it, their quarrels cease at once.

He who lives looking for pleasures only, his senses uncontrolled, immoderate in his food, idle, and weak, Mâra (the tempter) will certainly overthrow him, as the wind throws down a weak tree.

He who lives without looking for pleasures, his senses well

Source: from a translation by Max Muller found in *Sacred Books of the East*. Oxford University Press, 1900.

controlled, moderate in his food, faithful and strong, him Mâra will certainly not overthrow, any more than the wind throws down a rocky mountain.

He who wishes to put on the yellow dress (monk's robe) without having cleansed himself from sin, who disregards also temperance and truth, is unworthy of the yellow dress. But he who has cleansed himself from sin, is well grounded in all virtues, and endowed also with temperance and truth: he is indeed worthy of the yellow dress.

They who imagine truth in untruth, and see untruth in truth, never arrive at truth, but follow vain desires. They who know truth in truth, and untruth in untruth, arrive at truth, and follow true desires.

As rain breaks through an ill-thatched house, passion will break through an unreflecting mind. As rain does not break through a well-thatched house, passion will not break through a well-reflecting mind.

The evildoer mourns in this world, and he mourns in the next; he mourns in both. He mourns and suffers when he sees the evil result of his own work.

The virtuous man delights in this world, and he delights in the next; he delights in both. He delights and rejoices, when he sees the purity of his own work.

The evildoer suffers in this world, and he suffers in the next; he suffers in both. He suffers when he thinks of the evil he has done; he suffers more when going on the evil path.

The virtuous man is happy in this world, and he is happy in the next; he is happy in both. He is happy when he thinks of the good he has done; he is still more happy when going on the good path.

The thoughtless man, even if he can recite a large portion of the law, but is not a doer of it, has no share in the priesthood, but is like a cow-herd counting the cows of others.

The follower of the law, even if he can recite only a small portion of the law, but, having forsaken passion and hatred and foolishness, possesses true knowledge and serenity of mind, he, caring for nothing in this world or that to come, has indeed a share in the priesthood.

***

The Mind

As a fletcher makes straight his arrow, a wise man makes straight his trembling and unsteady thought, which is difficult to guard, difficult to hold back.

As a fish taken from his watery home and thrown on the dry ground, our thought trembles all over in order to escape the dominion of Mâra, the tempter.

It is good to tame the mind, which is difficult to hold in and flighty, rushing wherever it listeth; a tamed mind brings happiness.

Let the wise man guard his thoughts, for they are difficult to perceive, very artful, and they rush wherever they list: thoughts well-guarded bring happiness.

Those who bridle their mind which travels far, moves about alone, is without a body, and hides in the chamber of the heart, will be free from the bonds of Mâra, the tempter.

If a man's faith is unsteady, if he does not know the true law, if his peace of mind is troubled, his knowledge will never be perfect.

If a man's thoughts are not dissipated, if his mind is not perplexed, if he has ceased to think of good or evil, then there is no fear for him while he is watchful.

Knowing that this body is fragile like a jar, and making his thought firm like a fortress, one should attack Mâra, the tempter, with the weapon of knowledge, one should watch him when conquered, and should never rest.

Before long, alas! this body will lie on the earth, despised, without understanding, like a useless log.

Whatever a hater may do to a hater, or an enemy to an enemy, a wrongly-directed mind will do him greater mischief.

Not a mother, not a father, will do so much, nor any other relatives; a well-directed mind will do us greater service.

***

Nirvana (to Extinguish)

There is no suffering for him who has finished his journey, and abandoned grief, who has freed himself on all sides, and thrown off all fetters.

They exert themselves with their thoughts well-collected, they do not tarry in their abode; like swans who have left their lake, they leave their house and home.

Men who have no riches, who live on recognized food, who have perceived void and unconditioned freedom (Nirvana), their path is difficult to understand, like that of birds in the air.

He whose appetites are stilled, who is not absorbed in enjoyment, who has perceived void and unconditioned freedom (Nirvana), his path is difficult to understand, like that of birds in the air.

The gods even envy him whose senses, like horses well broken in by the driver, have been subdued, who is free from pride, and free from appetites; such a one who does his duty is tolerant like the earth, or like a threshold; he is like a lake without mud; no new births are in store for him.

His thought is quiet, quiet are his word and deed, when he has obtained freedom by true knowledge, when he has thus become a quiet man.

The man who is free from credulity, but knows the uncreated, who has cut all ties, removed all temptations, renounced all desires, he is the greatest of men.

In a hamlet or in a forest, on sea or on dry land, wherever venerable persons (Arhat) dwell, that place is delightful.

Forests are delightful; where the world finds no delight, there the passionless will find delight, for they look not for pleasures.

***

Selfish Craving (Tanha)

He who gives himself to vanity, and does not give himself to meditation, forgetting the real aim of life and grasping at pleasure, will in time envy him who has exerted himself in meditation.

Let no man ever cling to what is pleasant, or to what is unpleasant. Not to see what is pleasant is pain, and it is pain to see what is unpleasant.

Let, therefore, no man love anything; loss of the beloved is evil. Those who love nothing, and hate nothing, have no fetters. From pleasure comes grief, from pleasure comes fear; he who is free from pleasure knows neither grief nor fear.

From affection comes grief, from affection comes fear; he who is free from affection knows neither grief nor fear.

From lust comes grief, from lust comes fear; he who is free from lust knows neither grief nor fear.

From love comes grief, from love comes fear; he who is free from love knows neither grief nor fear.

From greed comes grief, from greed comes fear; he who is free from greed knows neither grief nor fear.

He who possesses virtue and intelligence, who is just, speaks the truth, and does what is his own business, him the world will hold dear.

He in whom a desire for the Ineffable (Nirvana) has sprung up, who in his mind is satisfied, and whose thoughts are not bewildered by love, he is called ûrdhvamsrotas (carried upwards by the stream).

Kinsmen, friends, and lovers salute a man who has been long away, and returns safe from afar.

In like manner his good works receive him who has done good, and has gone from this world to the other;—as kinsmen receive a friend on his return.

Part II:
Chinese Traditions

CHAPTER THREE

Confucianism

Teachings of Confucius
(Excerpts from the *Analects of Confucius*)

***

The Master said: Is he not *chün tzŭ* (the superior person)—he who is never concerned about status or fame? True *Jên* (virtue; benevolence) rarely goes with cunning speech and insinuating looks. At home, a young man should show the qualities of a son; abroad, those of a younger brother. He should be circumspect but truthful. He should have loving-kindness in his heart for all men, but associate only with the virtuous. After thus regulating his conduct, his surplus energy should be devoted to literary culture.

***

Tzŭ Kung inquired about the higher type of man. The Master replied: The higher type of man is one who acts before he speaks and professes only what he practices.

The Master said: The higher type of man is universal in his sympathy and free from party bias; the lower type of man is biased and un-sympathetic.

A man without loving-kindness in his heart—what has he to celebrate? A man without loving-kindness in his heart—what has he to sing about?

***

The chün tzŭ has three great virtues, which I cannot claim for myself. He is truly benevolent, and is free from care; he is truly wise, and is free from delusions; he is truly brave, and is free from fear. —Nay, replied Tzŭ Kung, these virtues are our Master's own.

Source: adapted from *The Sayings of Confucius,* translated by Lionel Giles. E. P. Dutton and Company, 1910.

***

Tzǔ Lu asked about the conduct of the chün tzǔ. The Master said: He cultivates himself so as to gain in self-respect.—Does he rest content with that?—He cultivates himself, was the reply, so as to give happiness to others.—And is he content with that?—He cultivates himself so as to confer peace and prosperity on the whole people.

By self-cultivation to confer peace and prosperity on the whole people!

***

It is the spirit of loving-kindness which makes a locality good to dwell in. He who selects a neighborhood without regard to this quality cannot be considered wise.

Only he who has the spirit of goodness within him is really able either to love or to hate.

The chün tzǔ never for a single instant quits the path of virtue; in times of storm and stress he remains in it as fast as ever.

The nobler sort of man in his progress through the world has neither narrow predilections nor obstinate antipathies. What he follows is the line of duty.

The nobler sort of man is proficient in the knowledge of his duty; the inferior man is proficient only in money-making.

***

Tzǔ Chang asked how to attain exalted virtue. ... The Master said: Make conscientiousness and truth your guiding principles, and thus pass on to the cultivation of duty to your neighbor. This is exalted virtue.

The Master said: The nobler sort of man emphasizes the good qualities in others and does not accentuate the bad. The inferior sort does the reverse.

***

The wise man will be slow to speak but quick to act.

***

Fan Ch'ih asked in what wisdom consisted. The Master said: Make righteousness in human affairs your aim, treat all supernatural beings with respect, but keep aloof from them— then you may be called wise. Asked about moral virtue, he replied: The virtuous man thinks of the difficult thing first and makes material advantage only a secondary consideration. This may be said to constitute moral virtue.

The Master said: The man of knowledge finds pleasure in the sea; the man of virtue finds pleasure in the mountains. For the man of knowledge is restless and the man of virtue is calm. The man of knowledge is happy, and the man of virtue is long-lived.

The higher type of man, having gathered wide objective knowledge from the branches of polite learning, will regulate the whole by the inner rule of conduct, and will thus avoid overstepping the limit.

That virtue is perfect which adheres to a constant mean. It has long been rare amongst men.

***

Better than one who knows what is right is one who is fond of what is right; and better than one who is fond of what is right is one who delights in what is right.

***

The higher type of man is calm and serene; the inferior man is constantly agitated and worried.

***

The Master said: The higher type of man makes a sense of duty the groundwork of his character, blends with it in action a sense of harmonious proportion, manifests it in a spirit of unselfishness, and perfects it by the addition of sincerity and truth. Then indeed is he a noble character.

The higher type of man seeks all that he wants in himself; the inferior man seeks all that he wants from others.

The higher type of man is firm but not quarrelsome; sociable, but not clannish.

***

The man of wisdom does not vacillate; the man of natural goodness does not fret; the man of valor does not fear.

***

The wise man does not esteem a person more highly because of what he says, neither does he undervalue what is said because of the person who says it.

***

Tzǔ Kung asked, saying: Is there any one maxim which ought to be acted upon throughout one's whole life?—The Master replied: Surely the maxim of loving-kindness is such:— Do not unto others what you would not they should do unto you.

***

Yen Yüan inquired as to the meaning of true goodness. The Master said: The subdual of self, and reversion to the natural laws governing conduct—this is true goodness. If a man can for the space of one day subdue his selfishness and revert to natural laws, the whole world will call him good. True goodness springs from a man's own heart. How can it depend on other men?— Yen Yüan said: Kindly tell me the practical rule to be deduced from this.—The Master replied: Do not use your eyes, your ears, your power of speech or your faculty of movement without obeying the inner law of self-control.—Yen Yüan said: Though I am not quick in thought or act, I will make it my business to carry out this precept.

Chung Kung inquired as to the meaning of true goodness. The Master said: When out of doors, behave as though you were entertaining a distinguished guest; in ruling the people, behave as though you were officiating at a solemn sacrifice; what you would not wish done to yourself, do not unto others. Then in public as in private life you will excite no ill-will. Chung Kung said: Though I am not quick in thought or act, I will make it my business to carry out this precept.

Ssŭ-ma Niu inquired as to the meaning of true goodness. The Master said: The truly good man is slow of speech.— Slowness of speech! Is this what goodness consists in?—The Master said: Does not the difficulty of deciding what it is right to *do* necessarily imply slowness to *speak*?

***

Mêng I Tzŭ asked for a definition of filial piety. The Master said: It consists in there being no falling off.— Fan Ch'ih said: What did you mean?—The Master replied: That parents should be served in the proper spirit while living, buried with the proper rites after death, and worshipped thereafter with the proper sacrifices.

Mêng Wu Po asked for a definition of filial piety. The Master said: There is filial piety when parents are spared all anxiety about their children except when they happen to fall sick.

Tzŭ Yu put a question on the subject of filial piety. The Master said: The filial piety of to-day reduces itself to the mere question of maintenance. Yet this is something in which even our dogs and horses have a share. Without the feeling of reverence, what is there to distinguish the two cases?

***

In serving his father and mother, a son may use gentle remonstrance; if he sees that they pay no heed, he should not desist, but merely increase in deference; if his pains are thrown away, he must show no resentment.

While one's parents are alive, one should not travel to a distance; if one must travel, it should be in a fixed direction.

The age of one's parents should always be kept in mind— on the one hand, as a subject for rejoicing; on the other, as a cause for alarm.

***

The Master said: To learn, and to practice on occasion what one has learnt—is this not true pleasure? The coming of a friend from a far-off land—is this not true joy?

***

Absorption in the study of the supernatural is most harmful.

***

Yu, shall I tell you what true knowledge is? When you know, to know that you know, and when you do not know, to know that you do not know—that is true knowledge.

***

When you see a good man, think of emulating him; when you see a bad man, examine your own heart.

CHAPTER FOUR
Taoism

Power of the Way

(Excerpts from *The Tao Te Ching*)

***

Ch. 1

The Tao (the Way) that can be spoken of
is not the unchanging Tao.
The name that can be named
is not the unchanging name.
Having no name,
it is the Source of heaven and earth.
Having a name,
it is the Mother of all things.

Always without desire we must be found,
If its deep mystery we would sound;
But if desire always within us be,
Its outer fringe is all that we shall see.

Under these two aspects,
it is really the same.
But as development takes place,
it receives the different names.
Together we call them the Mystery.

Where the Mystery is the deepest
is the gate of all that is subtle and wonderful.

Source: adapted from *The Tao Teh King*, by Lao-Tse. Translated by James Legge, 1891.

Ch. 2

All in the world know beauty,
and in doing this they know ugliness.
They all know the skill of the skillful,
and in doing this they know the want of skill.

Existence and non-existence give birth to one another.
Difficulty and ease produce the idea of the other.
Length and shortness fashion out the one the figure of the other.
High and low arise from the contrast of one with the other.
Notes and tones become harmonious through each other.
Before and after give the idea of one following another.

Thus, the sage manages affairs with non-action,
and conveys his instructions without the use of speech.

All things arise, and there is none which fails to show itself.
They grow, and there is no claim made for their ownership.
Going through their processes without expectation of reward.
Accomplishing without resting in achievement.

The work is done, but how no one can see;
'Tis this that makes the power not cease to be.

Ch. 3
Not to exalt those of superior ability
keeps the people from rivalry among themselves.
Not to prize rare things
is the way to keep them from becoming thieves.
Not to show them what is likely to excite their desires
is the way to keep their minds from disorder.

Thus the sage, in government the people,
empties their minds and fills their bellies,
weakens their wills and strengthens their bones.

He constantly aims to keep them without knowledge
    and without desire,
And to those with knowledge, keep them from acting upon it.

When there is this non-action, good order is universal.

Ch. 4
The Tao is like the emptiness of a vessel;
and while we employ it, we must guard against all fulness.
How deep and unfathomable it is,
as if it were the Honored Ancestor of all things!

We should blunt our sharp points,
and unravel the complications of things;
We should temper our brightness,
and bring ourselves into accord with the obscurity of others.

How pure and still the Tao is. It shall ever so continue!

I do not know whose son it is.
It might be older than God.

Ch. 5

The Tao does act from any wish to be benevolent;
it deals with all things as the dogs of grass are dealt with.
The sages do not act from any wish to be benevolent;
they deal with the people as the dogs of grass are dealt with.

May not the Tao be compared to a bellows?

'Tis emptied, yet it loses not its power;
'Tis moved again, and sends forth air the more.
Much speech to swift exhaustion lead we see;
Your inner being guard and keep it free.

Ch. 6

The Tao, the valley spirit, dies not.
It is thus named the female mystery.
Its gate, from which at first they issued forth,
is called the root from which grew heaven and earth.

Long and unbroken, the Tao's power remains,
used gently, and without the touch of pain.

Ch. 7
Heaven and earth are enduring
because they do not live of, or for, themselves.

Thus the sage puts herself last,
and yet she is always ahead.
She treats herself as if it were like any other,
and yet she is always preserved.

Is it not because she has no personal and private ends,
that therefore such ends are realized?

Ch. 8
The highest excellence is in being like water
which appears in its benefiting all things,
and in its occupying, without striving,
the low place which all men dislike.
hence its way is near to that of the Tao.

The excellence of a residence is in its suitability;
excellence of the mind is in abysmal stillness;
excellence of associations is in being with the virtuous;
excellence of government is in its securing good order;
excellence of work is in its productivity;
and that of any movement is in its timeliness.

And when one acts with highest excellence
without care of status
no one finds fault with him.

Ch. 9

It is better to leave a vessel unfilled,
than to attempt to carry it when it is full.

If you keep feeling a point that has been sharpened,
the point cannot long preserve its sharpness.

When gold and jade fill the hall,
their possessor cannot keep them safe.

When wealth and honors lead to arrogancy,
this brings its evil on itself.

When the work is done and one's name is becoming known,
to withdraw into obscurity is the way of Heaven.

Ch. 10

Holding the heart and mind together in one embrace,
can you keep them from separating?
Concentrating on your Chi (vital life force) breath to be soft,
can you become as a tender babe?
Cleansing away the most mysterious sights of your imagination,
can you become without flaw?
In loving the people and ruling the state,
can you proceed without any (purpose of) action?
In the opening and shutting of your gates of heaven,
can you do so as a female bird?
While your intelligence reaches in every direction,
can you appear to be without knowledge?

The Tao produces all things and nourishes them;
it produces them and does not claim them as its own;
it does all, and yet does not boast of it;
it presides over all, and yet does not control them.

This is the mysterious Te (inner power of the Tao).

Ch. 11

Thirty spokes unite in the one hub;
but it is on the empty space that the wheel depends.

Clay is fashioned into vessels;
but it is on their empty hollowness that their use depends.

Doors and windows are cut out from a wall to form a dwelling;
but it is on the empty space that its use depends.

Therefore, filling up serves for profit,
but emptiness is what makes it useful.

Ch. 14

We look, but cannot see it; and we name it 'the Equable.'
We listen, but cannot hear it, and we name it 'the Inaudible.'
We grasp, but cannot hold of it, and we name it 'the Subtle.'
With these three qualities, it avoids description;
and hence we blend them together and obtain The One.

Its upper part is not bright, and its lower part is not obscure.
Ceaseless in its action, it yet cannot be named,
and then it again returns and becomes nothing.
This is called the Form of the Formless,
and the Semblance of the Invisible;
this is called the Fleeting and Indeterminable.

We meet it and do not see its Front;
we follow it, and do not see its Back.

When we can take the Tao of old to direct the things of now,
and can know it as it was of old, in the beginning,
this is called (unwinding) the clue of Tao.

Ch. 15

The ancient masters, with exquisite penetration,
understood the mysteries of the Tao that eluded ordinary men.
What were they like?

Hesitant like those who wade through a stream in winter;
alert like those who are afraid of all around them;
humble like a guest to his host;
fluid like ice that is melting away;
unassuming like uncarved wood;
open like a valley;
and obscure like muddy water.

Who can make the muddy water clear?
Let it be still, and it will gradually become clear.
Who can secure the condition of rest?
Let movement flow and rest will gradually arise.

They who follow this method of the Tao do not wish to be full.
It is through their not being full
that they can afford to seem worn, old, and incomplete.

Ch. 16
Be empty.
Be still.

All things go through their processes of activity,
and then we see them return to their original state.
When vegetation has displayed luxuriant growth,
we see each of them return to its root.
This returning is called the state of stillness.
This stillness is the mark of fulfilling its purpose.

The mark of fulfilment is the unchanging rule.
To know that unchanging rule is to be intelligent.
Not to know it leads to chaos and difficulty.

Knowledge of that rule produces tolerance,
and that tolerance leads to a sense of community with all.
From this sense of community comes a kingliness of character;
and he who is king-like goes on to be heaven-like.
In that likeness to heaven he possesses the Tao.

Possessed of the Tao, he endures long;
and to the end of his bodily life,
is exempt from all danger of decay.

Ch. 19

If we could renounce our sageness
and discard our wisdom,
it would be better for the people a hundredfold.

If we could renounce our benevolence
and discard our righteousness,
the people would again become filial and kindly.

If we could renounce our artful contrivances
and discard our striving for gain,
there would be no thieves nor robbers.

Those three methods (of government)
Thought olden ways in elegance did fail
And made these names their want of worth to veil;
But simple views, and courses plain and true
Would selfish ends and many lusts eschew.

Ch. 22

The partial becomes complete;
the crooked, straight;
the empty, full;
the worn out, new.
He whose desires are few gets them;
he whose desires are many goes astray.

Thus the sage holds in his embrace the One thing,
and manifests it to all the world.
He is free from self-display, and therefore he shines;
from self-assertion, and therefore he is distinguished;
from self-boasting, and therefore his merit is acknowledged;
from self-complacency, and therefore he acquires superiority.
It is because he is free from striving
that no one in the world can strive with him.

That saying of the ancients, 'the partial becomes complete,'
was not vainly spoken:
—all real completion is comprehended under it.

Ch. 25

There was something undefined and complete,
coming into existence before Heaven and Earth.
How still it was and formless, standing alone, changeless,
reaching everywhere and without danger of depletion.
It may be regarded as the Mother of all things.

I do not know its name, so I call it the Tao (the Way).
Trying further to give it a name, I call it The Great.

Great, it passes on.
Passing on, it becomes remote.
Having become remote, it returns.
Thus the Tao is great;
Heaven is great;
Earth is great;
and the (sage) king is also great.
In the universe there are four that are great,
and the (sage) king is one of them.

Man takes his law from the Earth;
the Earth takes its law from Heaven;
Heaven takes its law from the Tao.
The law of the Tao is its being what it is.

Ch. 28

Who knows his manhood's strength,
Yet still his female feebleness maintains;
As to one channel flow the many drains,
All come to him, yea, all beneath the sky.
Thus he the constant excellence retains;
The simple child again, free from all stains.

Who knows how white attracts,
Yet always keeps himself within black's shade,
The pattern of humility displayed,
Displayed in view of all beneath the sky;
He in the unchanging excellence arrayed,
Endless return to man's first state has made.

Who knows how glory shines,
Yet loves disgrace, nor e'er for it is pale;
Behold his presence in a spacious vale,
To which men come from all beneath the sky.
The unchanging excellence completes its tale;
The simple infant man in him we hail.

All that is formed comes first from the unformed.
When placed in charge,
for her most important rules of state,
the sage employs no violent measures.

Ch. 29

If anyone should wish to get the kingdom for himself,
and to effect this by what he does,
I see that he will not succeed.

The kingdom is a spirit-like thing,
and cannot be got by active doing.
He who would so win it destroys it.
He who would hold it in his grasp loses it.

> *The course and nature of things is such that*
> *What was in front is now behind;*
> *What warmed anon we freezing find.*
> *Strength is of weakness oft the spoil;*
> *The store in ruins mocks our toil.*

Hence the sage:
puts away excessive effort,
extravagance,
and easy indulgence.

Thus the sage:
removes the extremes,
removes the extravagant and wasteful,
removes the arrogance.

Ch. 34
All-pervading is the Great Tao!
It may be found on the left hand and on the right.

All things depend on it for their production,
which it gives to them, not one refusing obedience to it.
When its work is accomplished,
it does not claim the name of having done it.
It clothes all things as with a garment,
and makes no assumption of being their lord;
—it may be named in the smallest things.
All things return (to their root and disappear),
and know not what presides over their doing so;
—it may be named in the greatest things.

Hence the sage can accomplish great things
by not making himself great.

Ch. 37
The Tao does nothing through action,
but through non-action all things are done.

If princes and kings were able to maintain it,
all things would naturally be transformed.

If this transformation became an object of desire,
you should express the desire by the nameless simplicity.

Simplicity without a name
Is free from all external aim.
With no desire, at rest and still,
All things go right as of their will.

Ch. 38

Those with great Te seek not to show it,
and therefore they possess it.
Those with feeble Te seek not to lose it,
and therefore they lack it.

Those with great Te do through non-action,
and have no need to do anything.
Those with feeble Te are always doing,
and have need to be so doing.

Those with great benevolence always seek to carry it out,
and have no need to be doing so.
Those with great righteousness always seek to carry it out,
and have need to be so doing.

Those with great propriety always seek to show it,
and if others fail to acknowledge it,
they seek to be acknowledged.

Thus it was that when the Tao was lost, Te appeared;
when Te was lost, benevolence appeared;
when benevolence was lost, righteousness appeared;
and when righteousness was lost, proprieties appeared.

Now propriety is the ghost of kindness and good faith,
and is also the origin of disorder.

Swift apprehension is a flower of the Tao,
and is the beginning of stupidity.

Thus the sage abides by what is solid,
and eschews what is flimsy;
dwells with the fruit and not with the flower.
She puts away the one and makes the choice of the other.

Ch. 40

The movement of the Tao, by contraries proceeds;
And weakness marks the course, of Tao's mighty deeds.

All things under heaven sprang from It
as existing and named.
That existence sprang from It
as non-existent and not named.

Ch. 42

The Tao produced One;
One produced Two;
Two produced Three;
Three produced All things.
All things leave behind them the Obscurity,
and go forward to embrace the Brightness,
while they are harmonized by the Chi of Vacancy.

What men dislike: to be orphaned, without virtue, directionless;
yet these are what kings and princes think of themselves.
So it is that some things are increased by being diminished,
and others are diminished by being increased.

What other men (thus) teach, I also teach.
The violent and strong do not die their natural death.
I will make this the basis of my teaching.

Ch. 43

The softest overcomes the hardest;
that which has no substance enters where there is no crevice.
This is the advantage that belongs to non-action.

Few in the world attain teaching without words,
and the advantage arising from non-action.

Ch. 48

Those devoted to knowledge, learn more each day.
Those devoted to the Tao, do less each day.

They diminish it again and again,
till they arrive at doing nothing.
Having arrived at this point of non-action,
there is nothing which they do not do.

He who gets as his own all under heaven
does so without giving himself grief.
If he gives himself grief,
he is not getting as his own all under heaven.

Ch. 51

All things come from the Tao,
are raised by the Te,
are shaped by their nature,
and are finalized by their circumstances.

Thus, all things honor the Tao, and exalt the Te.
This is not done through ordination,
but always as a spontaneous tribute.

The Tao begins them,
nourishes them, nurses them,
matures them, fulfills them,
brings them to their full growth,
maintains them and overspreads them.

It produces them without possessing them.
It births this process without boasting.
It carries them to completeness without controlling them;
—this is called the mysterious Te.

Ch. 63
Act through non-action.
Do through effortless doing.
Taste without discerning any flavor;
Consider what is small as great, and a few as many;
and recompense injury with kindness.

The sage plans for difficulty when something is easy,
and does great things while they are small.
All difficult things arise from the easy,
and all great things from the small.

Thus, the sage never does what is great,
but accomplishes the greatest things.

She who promises lightly
is sure to keep little faith.
She who expects everything to be easy
is sure to find many things difficult.

Thus, the sage plans for difficulty when something is easy,
and never experiences difficulty.

Ch. 71

To know, yet think we do not, is a healthy state.
Not to know, yet think we do, is a disease.

Pained by the thought of this disease
we are preserved from it.

The sage has not the disease.
She knows the pain that would be inseparable from it,
and thus she does not have it.

Ch. 76

Man at his birth is supple and weak;
at his death, firm and strong.
So it is with all things.
Trees and plants, in their early growth,
are soft and brittle;
at their death, dry and withered.

That firmness and strength are the results of death;
softness and weakness, the results of life.

He who relies on strength of his forces does not conquer;
but a tree which is strong will fill the out-stretched arms.

Thus the place of what is firm and strong is below,
and that of what is soft and weak is above.

Ch. 81

Sincere words are not precise.
Precise words are not sincere.
The sage need not argue their truth.
Those who need to argue are not sages.
Those who know the Tao are not extensively learned.
The extensively learned do not know the Tao.

The sage does not accumulate for himself.
The more that he expends for others,
the more does he possess of his own.
The more that he gives to others,
the more does he have himself.

With all the sharpness of the Way of Heaven,
it injures not.
With all the doing in the way of the sage,
he strives not.

Part III:
Abrahamic Traditions

CHAPTER FIVE
Judaism

Songs of God

(Excerpts from the book of *Psalms*)

***

Why standest Thou afar off, O LORD?
Why hidest Thou Thyself in times of trouble?
Through the pride of the wicked the poor is hotly pursued,
They are taken in the devices that they have imagined.
For the wicked boasteth of his heart's desire,
The covetous vaunts himself, though he condemns the LORD.
The wicked, in the pride of his countenance says 'He will not
    require';
All his thoughts are: 'There is no God.'

***

The heavens declare the glory of God,
And the firmament showeth His handiwork;
Day unto day uttereth speech,
And night unto night revealeth knowledge;
There is no speech, there are no words,
Neither is their voice heard.

...The law of the LORD is perfect, restoring the soul;
The testimony of the LORD is sure, making wise the simple.
The precepts of the LORD are right, rejoicing the heart;
The commandment of the LORD is pure, enlightening the eyes.
The fear of the LORD is clean, enduring forever;
The ordinances of the LORD are true, they are righteous
    altogether;
More to be desired are they than gold, yea, than much fine gold;
Sweeter also than honey and the honeycomb.

Source: *The Holy Scriptures* (Tanakh), translated and published by the Jewish Publication Society of America (JPS), 1917.

Moreover, by them is Thy servant warned;

***

Be still, and know that I am God.

***

How manifold are Thy works, O LORD!
In wisdom hast Thou made them all;
The earth is full of Thy creatures.
Yonder sea, great and wide,
Therein are creeping things innumerable,
Living creatures, both small and great.
There go the ships;
There is leviathan, whom Thou hast formed to sport therein.
All of them wait for Thee,
That Thou mayest give them their food in due season.
Thou givest it unto them, they gather it;
Thou openest Thy hand, they are satisfied with good.
Thou hidest Thy face, they vanish;
Thou withdrawest their breath, they perish,
And return to their dust.
Thou sendest forth Thy spirit, they are created;
And Thou renewest the face of the earth.

Wisdom of God

(Excerpts from the book of *Proverbs*)

***

The fear of the LORD is the beginning of knowledge;
But the foolish despise wisdom and discipline.

Wisdom crieth aloud in the streets,
She uttereth her voice in the broad places;
She calleth at the head of the noisy streets,
At the entrances of the gates, in the city, she uttereth her words:
'How long, ye thoughtless, will ye love thoughtlessness?
And how long will scorners delight them in scorning,
And fools hate knowledge?

***

My son, if thou wilt receive my words,
And lay up my commandments with thee;
So that thou make thine ear attend unto wisdom,
And thy heart incline to discernment;
Yea, if thou call for understanding,
And lift up thy voice for discernment;
If thou seek her as silver,
And search for her as for hid treasures;
Then shalt thou understand the fear of the LORD,
And find the knowledge of God.

***

Source: *The Holy Scriptures* (Tanakh), translated and published by the Jewish Publication Society of America (JPS), 1917.

My son, forget not my teaching;
But let thy heart keep my commandments;
For length of days, and years of life,
And peace, will they add to thee.
Let not kindness and truth forsake thee;
Bind them about thy neck,
write them upon the table of thy heart;
So shalt thou find grace and good favor
In the sight of God and man.
Trust in the LORD with all thy heart,
And lean not upon thine own understanding.
In all thy ways acknowledge Him,
And He will direct thy paths.
Be not wise in thine own eyes.

God's Intended Relationship with Man
(Excerpts from the book of *Genesis*)

***

And God saw everything that He had made, and, behold, it was very good.

Creation of all Things

In the beginning God created the heaven and the earth. Now the earth was unformed and void, and darkness was upon the face of the deep; and the spirit of God hovered over the face of the waters. And God said: 'Let there be light.' And there was light. And God saw the light, that it was good; and God divided the light from the darkness. And God called the light Day, and the darkness He called Night. And there was evening and there was morning, one day.

And God said: 'Let there be a firmament in the midst of the waters, and let it divide the waters from the waters.' And God made the firmament and divided the waters which were under the firmament from the waters which were above the firmament; and it was so. And God called the firmament Heaven. And there was evening and there was morning, a second day.

And God said: 'Let the waters under the heaven be gathered together unto one place, and let the dry land appear.' And it was so. And God called the dry land Earth, and the gathering together of the waters called He Seas; and God saw that it was good. And God said: 'Let the earth put forth grass, herb yielding seed, and fruit-tree bearing fruit after its kind, wherein is the seed thereof, upon the earth.' And it was so. And the earth brought forth grass, herb yielding seed after its kind, and tree bearing fruit, wherein is the seed thereof, after its kind; and God saw that

---

Source: *The Holy Scriptures* (Tanakh), translated and published by the Jewish Publication Society of America (JPS), 1917.

it was good. And there was evening and there was morning, a third day.

And God said: 'Let there be lights in the firmament of the heaven to divide the day from the night; and let them be for signs, and for seasons, and for days and years; and let them be for lights in the firmament of the heaven to give light upon the earth.' And it was so. And God made the two great lights: the greater light to rule the day, and the lesser light to rule the night; and the stars. And God set them in the firmament of the heaven to give light upon the earth, and to rule over the day and over the night, and to divide the light from the darkness; and God saw that it was good. And there was evening and there was morning, a fourth day.

And God said: 'Let the waters swarm with swarms of living creatures, and let fowl fly above the earth in the open firmament of heaven.' And God created the great sea-monsters, and every living creature that creepeth, wherewith the waters swarmed, after its kind, and every winged fowl after its kind; and God saw that it was good. And God blessed them, saying: 'Be fruitful, and multiply, and fill the waters in the seas, and let fowl multiply in the earth.' And there was evening and there was morning, a fifth day.

And God said: 'Let the earth bring forth the living creature after its kind, cattle, and creeping thing, and beast of the earth after its kind.' And it was so. And God made the beast of the earth after its kind, and the cattle after their kind, and every thing that creepeth upon the ground after its kind; and God saw that it was good. And God said: 'Let us make man in our image, after our likeness; and let them have dominion over the fish of the sea, and over the fowl of the air, and over the cattle, and over all the earth, and over every creeping thing that creepeth upon the earth.' And God created man in His own image, in the image of God created He him; male and female created He them. And God blessed them; and God said unto them: 'Be fruitful, and multiply, and replenish the earth, and subdue it; and have dominion over the fish of the sea, and over the fowl of the air, and over every living thing that creepeth upon the earth.' And God said: 'Behold, I have given you every herb yielding seed, which is upon the face of all the earth, and every tree, in which is the fruit of a tree yielding seed—to you it shall be for food; and to every beast of the earth, and to every fowl of the air, and to every thing that creepeth upon the earth, wherein there is a living soul, [I have given] every green herb for food.' And it was so. And God saw every thing that He had made, and, behold, it was very good. And there was evening and there was morning, the sixth day.

Man's Intended Home in Eden

And the heaven and the earth were finished, and all the host of them. And on the seventh day God finished His work which He had made; and He rested on the seventh day from all His work which He had made. And God blessed the seventh day and hallowed it; because that in it He rested from all His work which God in creating had made.

These are the generations of the heaven and of the earth when they were created, in the day that the LORD God made earth and heaven.

No shrub of the field was yet in the earth, and no herb of the field had yet sprung up; for the LORD God had not caused it to rain upon the earth, and there was not a man to till the ground; but there went up a mist from the earth, and watered the whole face of the ground. Then the LORD God formed man of the dust of the ground and breathed into his nostrils the breath of life; and man became a living soul. And the LORD God planted a garden eastward, in Eden; and there He put the man whom He had formed. And out of the ground made the LORD God to grow every tree that is pleasant to the sight, and good for food; the tree of life also in the midst of the garden, and the tree of the knowledge of good and evil. And a river went out of Eden to water the garden; and from thence it was parted and became four heads. The name of the first is Pishon; that is it which compasses the whole land of Havilah, where there is gold; and the gold of that land is good; there is bdellium and the onyx stone. And the name of the second river is Gihon; the same is it that compassed the whole land of Cush. And the name of the third river is Tigris; that is it which goeth toward the east of Asshur. And the fourth river is the Euphrates. And the LORD God took the man and put him into the garden of Eden to dress it and to keep it. And the LORD God commanded the man, saying: 'Of every tree of the garden thou mayest freely eat; but of the tree of the knowledge of good and evil, thou shalt not eat of it; for in the day that thou eatest thereof thou shalt surely die.'

And the LORD God said: 'It is not good that the man should be alone; I will make him a help meet for him.' And out of the ground the LORD God formed every beast of the field, and every fowl of the air; and brought them unto the man to see what he would call them; and whatsoever the man would call every living creature, that was to be the name thereof. And the man gave names to all cattle, and to the fowl of the air, and to every beast of the field; but for Adam there was not found a help meet for him. And the LORD God caused a deep sleep to fall upon the man, and he slept; and He took one of his ribs and closed up the place with flesh instead thereof. And the rib, which the LORD God had taken from the man, made He a woman, and brought her unto the man. And the man said: 'This is now bone of my bones, and flesh of my flesh; she shall be called Woman, because she was taken out of Man.' Therefore, shall a man leave his father and his mother, and shall cleave unto his wife, and they shall be one flesh. And they were both naked, the man and his wife, and were not ashamed.

Choosing Knowledge of Good & Evil

Now the serpent was more subtle than any beast of the field

which the LORD God had made. And he said unto the woman: 'Yea, hath God said: Ye shall not eat of any tree of the garden?' And the woman said unto the serpent: 'Of the fruit of the trees of the garden we may eat; but of the fruit of the tree which is in the midst of the garden, God hath said: Ye shall not eat of it, neither shall ye touch it, lest ye die.' And the serpent said unto the woman: 'Ye shall not surely die; for God doth know that in the day ye eat thereof, then your eyes shall be opened, and ye shall be as God, knowing good and evil.' And when the woman saw that the tree was good for food, and that it was a delight to the eyes, and that the tree was to be desired to make one wise, she took of the fruit thereof, and did eat; and she gave also unto her husband with her, and he did eat. And the eyes of them both were opened, and they knew that they were naked; and they sewed fig-leaves together and made themselves girdles. And they heard the voice of the LORD God walking in the garden toward the cool of the day; and the man and his wife hid themselves from the presence of the LORD God amongst the trees of the garden. And the LORD God called unto the man, and said unto him: 'Where art thou?' And he said: 'I heard Thy voice in the garden, and I was afraid, because I was naked; and I hid myself.' And He said: 'Who told thee that thou wast naked? Hast thou eaten of the tree, whereof I commanded thee that thou shouldest not eat?' And the man said: 'The woman whom Thou gavest to be with me, she gave me of the tree, and I did eat.' And the LORD God said unto the woman: 'What is this thou hast done?' And the woman said: 'The serpent beguiled me, and I did eat.' And the LORD God said unto the serpent: 'Because thou hast done this, cursed art thou from among all cattle, and from among all beasts of the field; upon thy belly shalt thou go, and dust shalt thou eat all the days of thy life. And I will put enmity between thee and the woman, and between thy seed and her seed; they shall bruise thy head, and thou shalt bruise their heel.'

Unto the woman He said: 'I will greatly multiply thy pain and thy travail; in pain thou shalt bring forth children; and thy desire shall be to thy husband, and he shall rule over thee.'

And unto Adam He said: 'Because thou hast hearkened unto the voice of thy wife, and hast eaten of the tree, of which I commanded thee, saying: Thou shalt not eat of it; cursed is the ground for thy sake; in toil shalt thou eat of it all the days of thy life. Thorns also and thistles shall it bring forth to thee; and thou shalt eat the herb of the field. In the sweat of thy face shalt thou eat bread, till thou return unto the ground; for out of it wast thou taken; for dust thou art, and unto dust shalt thou return.' And the man called his wife's name Eve; because she was the mother of all living. And the LORD God made for Adam and for his wife garments of skins and clothed them.

And the LORD God said: 'Behold, the man is become as one of us, to know good and evil; and now, lest he put forth his hand, and take also of the tree of life, and eat, and live forever.' Therefore, the LORD God sent him forth from the garden of Eden, to till the ground from whence he was taken. So He drove out the man; and He placed at the east of the garden of Eden the cherubim, and the flaming sword which turned every way, to keep the way to the tree of life.

Saving Life from the Wicked

(Excerpts from the book of *Genesis*)

***

Noah's Ark

And it came to pass, when men began to multiply on the face of the earth, and daughters were born unto them, that the sons of God saw the daughters of men that they were fair; and they took them wives, whomsoever they chose.

...And the LORD saw that the wickedness of man was great in the earth, and that every imagination of the thoughts of his heart was only evil continually. And it repented the LORD that He had made man on the earth, and it grieved Him at His heart. And the LORD said: 'I will blot out man whom I have created from the face of the earth; both man, and beast, and creeping thing, and fowl of the air; for it repenteth Me that I have made them.' But Noah found grace in the eyes of the LORD.

... And the earth was corrupt before God, and the earth was filled with violence. And God saw the earth, and, behold, it was corrupt; for all flesh had corrupted their way upon the earth. And God said unto Noah: 'The end of all flesh is come before Me; for the earth is filled with violence through them; and, behold, I will destroy them with the earth. Make thee an ark of gopher wood... And I, behold, I do bring the flood of waters upon the earth, to destroy all flesh, wherein is the breath of life, from under heaven; every thing that is in the earth shall perish. But I will establish My covenant with thee; and thou shalt come into the ark, thou, and thy sons, and thy wife, and thy sons' wives with thee. And of every living thing of all flesh, two of every sort shalt thou bring into the ark, to keep them alive with thee; they shall be male and female.

Source: *The Holy Scriptures* (Tanakh), translated and published by the Jewish Publication Society of America (JPS), 1917.

The Flood of Re-creation

And Noah was six hundred years old when the flood of waters was upon the earth... And it came to pass after the seven days, that the waters of the flood were upon the earth.

And the flood was forty days upon the earth; and the waters increased, and bore up the ark, and it was lifted up above the earth. And the waters prevailed and increased greatly upon the earth; and the ark went upon the face of the waters. And the waters prevailed exceedingly upon the earth; and all the high mountains that were under the whole heaven were covered...

And God remembered Noah, and every living thing, and all the cattle that were with him in the ark; and God made a wind to pass over the earth, and the waters assuaged; the fountains also of the deep and the windows of heaven were stopped, and the rain from heaven was restrained. And the waters returned from off the earth continually; and after the end of a hundred and fifty days the waters decreased. And the ark rested in the seventh month, on the seventeenth day of the month, upon the mountains of Ararat. And the waters decreased continually until the tenth month; in the tenth month, on the first day of the month, were the tops of the mountains seen.

And God spoke unto Noah, saying: 'Go forth from the ark, thou, and thy wife, and thy sons, and thy sons' wives with thee. Bring forth with thee every living thing that is with thee of all flesh, both fowl, and cattle, and every creeping thing that creepeth upon the earth; that they may swarm in the earth, and be fruitful, and multiply upon the earth.' And Noah went forth, and his sons, and his wife, and his sons' wives with him; every beast, every creeping thing, and every fowl, whatsoever moveth upon the earth, after their families; went forth out of the ark.

And Noah builded an altar unto the LORD; and took of every clean beast, and of every clean fowl, and offered burnt-offerings on the altar. And the LORD smelled the sweet savor;

and the LORD said in His heart: 'I will not again curse the ground any more for man's sake; for the imagination of man's heart is evil from his youth; neither will I again smite any more every thing living, as I have done. While the earth remaineth, seedtime and harvest, and cold and heat, and summer and winter, and day and night shall not cease.'

God's Promise of Faith
(Excerpts from the book of *Genesis*)

***

The sons of Noah who came out of the ark were Shem, Ham and Japheth. Terah, a descendant of Shem, was the father of Abraham, Nahor and Haran; and Haran was the father of Lot...

Answering God's Call

Now the LORD said unto Abram: 'Get thee out of thy country, and from thy kindred, and from thy father's house, unto the land that I will show thee. And I will make of thee a great nation, and I will bless thee, and make thy name great; and be thou a blessing. And I will bless them that bless thee, and him that curseth thee will I curse; and in thee shall all the families of the earth be blessed.' So Abram went, as the LORD had spoken unto him; and Lot went with him; and Abram was seventy and five years old when he departed out of Haran. And Abram took Sarai his wife, and Lot his brother's son, and all their substance that they had gathered, and the souls that they had gotten in Haran; and they went forth...

...And Abram was very rich in cattle, in silver, and in gold. And he went on his journeys from the South even to Beth-el, unto the place where his tent had been at the beginning, between Beth-el and Ai; unto the place of the altar, which he had made there at the first; and Abram called there on the name of the LORD. And Lot also, who went with Abram, had flocks, and herds, and tents. And the land was not able to bear them, that they might dwell together; for their substance was great, so that

---

Source: *The Holy Scriptures* (Tanakh), translated and published by the Jewish Publication Society of America (JPS), 1917.

they could not dwell together…

…And the LORD said unto Abram, after that Lot was separated from him: 'Lift up now thine eyes, and look from the place where thou art, northward and southward and eastward and westward; for all the land which thou seest, to thee will I give it, and to thy seed forever. And I will make thy seed as the dust of the earth; so that if a man can number the dust of the earth, then shall thy seed also be numbered. Arise, walk through the land in the length of it and in the breadth of it; for unto thee will I give it.' And Abram moved his tent, and came and dwelt by the terebinths of Mamre, which are in Hebron, and built there an altar unto the LORD.

And it came to pass in the days of Amraphel king of Shinar, Arioch king of Ellasar, Chedorlaomer king of Elam, and Tidal king of Goiim, that they made war with Bera king of Sodom, and with Birsha king of Gomorrah, Shinab king of Admah, and Shemeber king of Zeboiim, and the king of Bela— And they took all the goods of Sodom and Gomorrah, and all their victuals, and went their way. And they took Lot, Abram's brother's son, who dwelt in Sodom, and his goods, and departed… And when Abram heard that his brother was taken captive, he led forth his trained men, born in his house, three hundred and eighteen, and pursued as far as Dan. And he divided himself against them by night, he and his servants, and smote them, and pursued them unto Hobah, which is on the left hand of Damascus. And he brought back all the goods, and also brought back his brother Lot, and his goods, and the women also, and the people… And Melchizedek king of Salem brought forth bread and wine; and he was priest of God the Most High. And he blessed him and said: 'Blessed be Abram of God Most High, Maker of heaven and earth; and blessed be God the Most High, who hath delivered thine enemies into thy hand.' And he gave him a tenth of all.

After these things the word of the LORD came unto Abram

in a vision, saying: 'Fear not, Abram, I am thy shield, thy reward shall be exceeding great.' And Abram said: 'O Lord GOD, what wilt Thou give me, seeing I go hence childless, and he that shall be possessor of my house is Eliezer of Damascus?' And Abram said: 'Behold, to me Thou hast given no seed, and, lo, one born in my house is to be mine heir.' And, behold, the word of the LORD came unto him, saying: 'This man shall not be thine heir; but he that shall come forth out of thine own bowels shall be thine heir.' And He brought him forth abroad, and said: 'Look now toward heaven, and count the stars, if thou be able to count them'; and He said unto him: 'So shall thy seed be.' And he believed in the LORD; and He counted it to him for righteousness. And He said unto him: 'I am the LORD that brought thee out of Ur of the Chaldees, to give thee this land to inherit it…And it came to pass, that, when the sun was going down, a deep sleep fell upon Abram; and, lo, a dread, even a great darkness, fell upon him. And He said unto Abram: 'Know of a surety that thy seed shall be a stranger in a land that is not theirs, and shall serve them; and they shall afflict them four hundred years; and also that nation, whom they shall serve, will I judge; and afterward shall they come out with great substance. But thou shalt go to thy fathers in peace; thou shalt be buried in a good old age. And in the fourth generation they shall come back hither; for the iniquity of the Amorite is not yet full.' And it came to pass, that, when the sun went down, and there was thick darkness, behold a smoking furnace, and a flaming torch that passed between these pieces. In that day the LORD made a covenant with Abram, saying: 'Unto thy seed have I given this land, from the river of Egypt unto the great river, the river Euphrates; the Kenite, and the Kenizzite, and the Kadmonite, and the Hittite, and the Perizzite, and the Rephaim, and the Amorite, and the Canaanite, and the Girgashite, and the Jebusite.'

The Faith of Hagar: Birth of Ishmael

Now Sarai Abram's wife bore him no children; and she had a handmaid, an Egyptian, whose name was Hagar. And Sarai said unto Abram: 'Behold now, the LORD hath restrained me from bearing; go in, I pray thee, unto my handmaid; it may be that I shall be built up through her.' And Abram hearkened to the voice of Sarai. And Sarai Abram's wife took Hagar the Egyptian, her handmaid, after Abram had dwelt ten years in the land of Canaan and gave her to Abram her husband to be his wife. And he went in unto Hagar, and she conceived; and when she saw that she had conceived, her mistress was despised in her eyes. And Sarai said unto Abram: 'My wrong be upon thee: I gave my handmaid into thy bosom; and when she saw that she had conceived, I was despised in her eyes: the LORD judge between me and thee.' But Abram said unto Sarai: 'Behold, thy maid is in thy hand; do to her that which is good in thine eyes.' And Sarai dealt harshly with her, and she fled from her face. And the angel of the LORD found her by a fountain of water in the wilderness, by the fountain in the way to Shur. And he said: 'Hagar, Sarai's handmaid, whence camest thou? and whither goest thou?' And she said: 'I flee from the face of my mistress Sarai.' And the angel of the LORD said unto her: 'Return to thy mistress and submit thyself under her hands.' And the angel of the LORD said unto her: 'I will greatly multiply thy seed, that it shall not be numbered for multitude. And the angel of the LORD said unto her: 'Behold, thou art with child, and shalt bear a son; and thou shalt call his name Ishmael, because the LORD hath heard thy affliction. And he shall be a wild ass of a man: his hand shall be against every man, and every man's hand against him; and he shall dwell in the face of all his brethren.' And she called the name of the LORD that spoke unto her, Thou art a God of seeing; for she said: 'Have I even here seen Him that seeth Me?'...

Faith of a New Life: Birth of Isaac

...And when Abram was ninety years old and nine, the LORD appeared to Abram, and said unto him: 'I am God Almighty; walk before Me and be thou wholehearted. And I will make My covenant between Me and thee, and will multiply thee exceedingly.' And Abram fell on his face; and God talked with him, saying: 'As for Me, behold, My covenant is with thee, and thou shalt be the father of a multitude of nations. Neither shall thy name any more be called Abram, but thy name shall be Abraham; for the father of a multitude of nations have I made thee. And I will make thee exceeding fruitful, and I will make nations of thee, and kings shall come out of thee. And I will establish My covenant between Me and thee and thy seed after thee throughout their generations for an everlasting covenant, to be a God unto thee and to thy seed after thee. And I will give unto thee, and to thy seed after thee, the land of thy sojourning, all the land of Canaan, for an everlasting possession; and I will be their God.' And God said unto Abraham: 'And as for thee, thou shalt keep My covenant, thou, and thy seed after thee throughout their generations. This is My covenant, which ye shall keep, between Me and you and thy seed after thee: every male among you shall be circumcised. And ye shall be circumcised in the flesh of your foreskin; and it shall be a token of a covenant betwixt Me and you. And he that is eight days old shall be circumcised among you, every male throughout your generations, he that is born in the house, or bought with money of any foreigner, that is not of thy seed. He that is born in thy house, and he that is bought with thy money, must needs be circumcised; and My covenant shall be in your flesh for an everlasting covenant. And the uncircumcised male who is not circumcised in the flesh of his foreskin, that soul shall be cut off from his people; he hath broken My covenant.'

And God said unto Abraham: 'As for Sarai thy wife, thou

shalt not call her name Sarai, but Sarah shall her name be. And I will bless her, and moreover I will give thee a son of her; yea, I will bless her, and she shall be a mother of nations; kings of peoples shall be of her.' Then Abraham fell upon his face, and laughed, and said in his heart: 'Shall a child be born unto him that is a hundred years old? and shall Sarah, that is ninety years old, bear?' And Abraham said unto God: 'Oh that Ishmael might live before Thee!' And God said: 'Nay, but Sarah thy wife shall bear thee a son; and thou shalt call his name Isaac; and I will establish My covenant with him for an everlasting covenant for his seed after him. And as for Ishmael, I have heard thee; behold, I have blessed him, and will make him fruitful, and will multiply him exceedingly; twelve princes shall he beget, and I will make him a great nation. But My covenant will I establish with Isaac, whom Sarah shall bear unto thee at this set time in the next year.' And He left off talking with him, and God went up from Abraham...

...Now Abraham and Sarah were old, and well stricken in age; it had ceased to be with Sarah after the manner of women.— And Sarah laughed within herself, saying: 'After I am waxed old shall I have pleasure, my lord being old also?' And the LORD said unto Abraham: 'Wherefore did Sarah laugh, saying: Shall I of a surety bear a child, who am old? Is anything too hard for the LORD. At the set time I will return unto thee, when the season cometh round, and Sarah shall have a son.' Then Sarah denied, saying: 'I laughed not'; for she was afraid. And He said: 'Nay; but thou didst laugh.'

And the LORD remembered Sarah as He had said, and the LORD did unto Sarah as He had spoken. And Sarah conceived, and bore Abraham a son in his old age, at the set time of which God had spoken to him. And Abraham called the name of his son that was born unto him, whom Sarah bore to him, Isaac. And Abraham circumcised his son Isaac when he was eight days old, as God had commanded him. And Abraham was a hundred years old, when his son Isaac was born unto him. And Sarah said: 'God hath made laughter for me; everyone that heareth will laugh on account of me.' And she said: 'Who would have said unto Abraham, that Sarah should give children suck? for I have borne him a son in his old age.'

Test of Faith: The Sacrifice of Isaac

And it came to pass after these things, that God did prove Abraham, and said unto him: 'Abraham'; and he said: 'Here am I.' And He said: 'Take now thy son, thine only son, whom thou lovest, even Isaac, and get thee into the land of Moriah; and offer him there for a burnt-offering upon one of the mountains which I will tell thee of.' And Abraham rose early in the morning, and saddled his ass, and took two of his young men with him, and Isaac his son; and he cleaved the wood for the burnt-offering, and rose up, and went unto the place of which God had told him.

On the third day Abraham lifted up his eyes and saw the place afar off. And Abraham said unto his young men: 'Abide ye here with the ass, and I and the lad will go yonder; and we will worship and come back to you.' And Abraham took the wood of the burnt-offering and laid it upon Isaac his son; and he took in his hand the fire and the knife; and they went both of them together. And Isaac spoke unto Abraham his father and said: 'My father.' And he said: 'Here am I, my son.' And he said: 'Behold the fire and the wood; but where is the lamb for a burnt-offering?' And Abraham said: 'God will provide Himself the lamb for a burnt-offering, my son.'

So they went both of them together. And they came to the place which God had told him of; and Abraham built the altar there, and laid the wood in order, and bound Isaac his son, and laid him on the altar, upon the wood. And Abraham stretched forth his hand and took the knife to slay his son. And the angel of the LORD called unto him out of heaven, and said:

'Abraham, Abraham.' And he said: 'Here am I.' And he said: 'Lay not thy hand upon the lad, neither do thou anything unto him; for now I know that thou art a God-fearing man, seeing thou hast not withheld thy son, thine only son, from Me.' And Abraham lifted up his eyes, and looked, and behold behind him a ram caught in the thicket by his horns. And Abraham went and took the ram and offered him up for a burnt-offering in the stead of his son. And Abraham called the name of that place Adonai-jireh; as it is said to this day: 'In the mount where the LORD is seen.' And the angel of the LORD called unto Abraham a second time out of heaven, and said: 'By Myself have I sworn, saith the LORD, because thou hast done this thing, and hast not withheld thy son, thine only son, that in blessing I will bless thee, and in multiplying I will multiply thy seed as the stars of the heaven, and as the sand which is upon the seashore; and thy seed shall possess the gate of his enemies; and in thy seed shall all the nations of the earth be blessed; because thou hast hearkened to My voice.'

Wrestling with God
(Excerpts from the book of *Genesis*)

***

The Birth of Israel
A story of Jacob, son of Isaac

...And Jacob went on his way, and the angels of God met him. And Jacob said when he saw them: 'This is God's camp.' And he called the name of that place Mahanaim...

...And he rose up that night, and took his two wives, and his two handmaids, and his eleven children, and passed over the ford of the Jabbok. And he took them, and sent them over the stream, and sent over that which he had. And Jacob was left alone; and there wrestled a man with him until the breaking of the day. And when he saw that he prevailed not against him, he touched the hollow of his thigh; and the hollow of Jacob's thigh was strained, as he wrestled with him. And he said: 'Let me go, for the day breaketh.' And he said: 'I will not let thee go, except thou bless me.' And he said unto him: 'What is thy name?' And he said: 'Jacob.' And he said: 'Thy name shall be called no more Jacob, but Israel; for thou hast striven with God and with men, and hast prevailed.' And Jacob asked him, and said: 'Tell me, I pray thee, thy name.' And he said: 'Wherefore is it that thou dost ask after my name?' And he blessed him there. And Jacob called the name of the place Peniel: 'for I have seen God face to face, and my life is preserved.' And the sun rose upon him as he passed over Peniel, and he limped upon his thigh.

Source: *The Holy Scriptures* (Tanakh), translated and published by the Jewish Publication Society of America (JPS), 1917.

The Name of God

(Excerpts from the book of *Exodus*)

After leaving their land due to a famine, the sons and daughters of Israel (the Israelites) migrate to Egypt and multiply. They are eventually oppressed, enslaved by a new Pharaoh (king), who commanded all their male children to be killed.

Moses is called by God to save them.

***

Now Moses was keeping the flock of Jethro his father-in-law, the priest of Midian; and he led the flock to the farthest end of the wilderness, and came to the mountain of God, unto Horeb. And the angel of the LORD appeared unto him in a flame of fire out of the midst of a bush; and he looked, and, behold, the bush burned with fire, and the bush was not consumed.

And Moses said: 'I will turn aside now, and see this great sight, why the bush is not burnt.'

And when the LORD saw that he turned aside to see, God called unto him out of the midst of the bush, and said: 'Moses, Moses.' And he said: 'Here am I.' And He said: 'Draw not nigh hither; put off thy shoes from off thy feet, for the place whereon thou standest is holy ground.' Moreover He said: 'I am the God of thy father, the God of Abraham, the God of Isaac, and the God of Jacob.'

And Moses hid his face; for he was afraid to look upon God. And the LORD said: 'I have surely seen the affliction of My people that are in Egypt, and have heard their cry by reason of their taskmasters; for I know their pains; and I am come down to deliver them out of the hand of the Egyptians, and to bring

Source: *The Holy Scriptures* (Tanakh), translated and published by the Jewish Publication Society of America (JPS), 1917.

them up out of that land unto a good land and a large, unto a land flowing with milk and honey; unto the place of the Canaanite, and the Hittite, and the Amorite, and the Perizzite, and the Hivite, and the Jebusite. And now, behold, the cry of the children of Israel is come unto Me; moreover I have seen the oppression wherewith the Egyptians oppress them. Come now therefore, and I will send thee unto Pharaoh, that thou mayest bring forth My people the children of Israel out of Egypt.'

And Moses said unto God: 'Who am I, that I should go unto Pharaoh, and that I should bring forth the children of Israel out of Egypt?'

And He said: 'Certainly I will be with thee; and this shall be the token unto thee, that I have sent thee: when thou hast brought forth the people out of Egypt, ye shall serve God upon this mountain.'

And Moses said unto God: 'Behold, when I come unto the children of Israel, and shall say unto them: The God of your fathers hath sent me unto you; and they shall say to me: What is His name? what shall I say unto them?'

And God said unto Moses: 'I AM THAT I AM'; and He said: 'Thus shalt thou say unto the children of Israel: I AM hath sent me unto you.' And God said moreover unto Moses: 'Thus shalt thou say unto the children of Israel: The LORD, the God of your fathers, the God of Abraham, the God of Isaac, and the God of Jacob, hath sent me unto you; this is My name for ever, and this is My memorial unto all generations. Go, and gather the elders of Israel together, and say unto them: The LORD, the God of your fathers, the God of Abraham, of Isaac, and of Jacob, hath appeared unto me, saying: I have surely remembered you, and seen that which is done to you in Egypt. And I have said: I will bring you up out of the affliction of Egypt unto the land of the Canaanite, and the Hittite, and the Amorite, and the Perizzite, and the Hivite, and the Jebusite, unto a land flowing with milk and honey

Commandments of God

(Excerpts from the book of *Exodus*)

After helping free the Israelites from Egypt, Moses begins leading them on a long, arduous journey to God's promised land.

***

In the third month after the children of Israel were gone forth out of the land of Egypt, the same day came they into the wilderness of Sinai...

...the LORD came down upon mount Sinai, to the top of the mount; and the LORD called Moses to the top of the mount; and Moses went up. And the LORD said unto Moses: 'Go down, charge the people, lest they break through unto the LORD to gaze, and many of them perish. And let the priests also, that come near to the LORD, sanctify themselves, lest the LORD break forth upon them.' And Moses said unto the LORD: 'The people cannot come up to mount Sinai; for thou didst charge us, saying: Set bounds about the mount, and sanctify it.' And the LORD said unto him: 'Go, get thee down, and thou shalt come up, thou, and Aaron with thee; but let not the priests and the people break through to come up unto the LORD, lest He break forth upon them.' So Moses went down unto the people, and told them.

And God spoke all these words, saying:
I am the LORD thy God, who brought thee out of the land of Egypt, out of the house of bondage. Thou shalt have no other gods before Me.
Thou shalt not make unto thee a graven image, nor any manner of likeness, of anything that is in heaven above, or that is in the earth beneath, or that is in the water under the earth;

Source: *The Holy Scriptures* (Tanakh), translated and published by the Jewish Publication Society of America (JPS), 1917.

thou shalt not bow down unto them, nor serve them; for I the LORD thy God am a jealous God, visiting the iniquity of the fathers upon the children unto the third and fourth generation of them that hate Me; and showing mercy unto the thousandth generation of them that love Me and keep My commandments.

Thou shalt not take the name of the LORD thy God in vain; for the LORD will not hold him guiltless that taketh His name in vain.

Remember the sabbath day, to keep it holy. Six days shalt thou labor, and do all thy work; but the seventh day is a sabbath unto the LORD thy God, in it thou shalt not do any manner of work, thou, nor thy son, nor thy daughter, nor thy man-servant, nor thy maid-servant, nor thy cattle, nor thy stranger that is within thy gates; for in six days the LORD made heaven and earth, the sea, and all that in them is, and rested on the seventh day; wherefore the LORD blessed the sabbath day, and hallowed it.

Honor thy father and thy mother, that thy days may be long upon the land which the LORD thy God giveth thee.

Thou shalt not murder.

Thou shalt not commit adultery.

Thou shalt not steal.

Thou shalt not bear false witness against thy neighbor.

Thou shalt not covet thy neighbor's house; thou shalt not covet thy neighbor's wife, nor his man-servant, nor his maid-servant, nor his ox, nor his ass, nor any thing that is thy neighbor's.

And all the people perceived the thundering, and the lightnings, and the voice of the horn, and the mountain smoking; and when the people saw it, they trembled, and stood afar off. And they said unto Moses: 'Speak thou with us, and we will hear; but let not God speak with us, lest we die.' And Moses said unto the people: 'Fear not; for God is come to prove you, and that His fear may be before you, that ye sin not.' And the people stood afar off; but Moses drew near unto the thick darkness where God was.

And the LORD said unto Moses: Thus thou shalt say unto the children of Israel: Ye yourselves have seen that I have talked with you from heaven. Ye shall not make with Me—gods of silver, or gods of gold, ye shall not make unto you. An altar of earth thou shalt make unto Me, and shalt sacrifice thereon thy burnt-offerings, and thy peace-offerings, thy sheep, and thine oxen; in every place where I cause My name to be mentioned I will come unto thee and bless thee. And if thou make Me an altar of stone, thou shalt not build it of hewn stones; for if thou lift up thy tool upon it, thou hast profaned it. Neither shalt thou go up by steps unto Mine altar, that thy nakedness be not uncovered thereon.

CHAPTER SIX

Christianity

The Son of God
(Excerpts from the books of *Matthew and Mark*)

***

From Abraham to Jesus

The book of the generation of Jesus Christ, the son of David, the son of Abraham:

Abraham begot Isaac. And Isaac begot Jacob. And Jacob begot Judas and his brethren...

...And Eleazar begot Mathan. And Mathan begot Jacob. And Jacob begot Joseph the husband of Mary, of whom was born Jesus, who is called Christ.

So all the generations from Abraham to David, are fourteen generations. And from David to the transmigration of Babylon, are fourteen generations: and from the transmigration of Babylon to Christ are fourteen generations.

The Pure Birth of Jesus

Now the generation of Christ was in this wise. When as his mother Mary was espoused to Joseph, before they came together, she was found with child, of the Holy Ghost. Whereupon Joseph her husband, being a just man, and not willing publicly to expose her, was minded to put her away privately. But while he thought on these things, behold the Angel of the Lord appeared to him in his sleep, saying: Joseph, son of David, fear not to take unto thee Mary thy wife, for that which is conceived in her, is of the Holy Ghost. And she shall bring forth a son: and thou shalt call his name Jesus. For he shall save his people from their sins. Now all this was done that it might be fulfilled which the Lord spoke by the prophet, saying: Behold a

Source: *Douay-Rheims Bible* (DRB) with Bishop Challoner revision, 1752.

virgin shall be with child, and bring forth a son, and they shall call his name Emmanuel, which being interpreted is, God with us. And Joseph rising up from sleep, did as the angel of the Lord had commanded him, and took unto him his wife. And he knew her not, till she brought forth her first born son: and he called his name Jesus.

Preaching the Good News

...Jesus came in Galilee, preaching the gospel of the kingdom of God, And saying: The time is accomplished and the kingdom of God is at hand. Repent and believe the gospel.

...And there was in their synagogue a man with an unclean spirit; and he cried out, Saying: What have we to do with thee, Jesus of Nazareth? Art thou come to destroy us? I know who thou art, the Holy One of God. And Jesus threatened him, saying: Speak no more, and go out of the man. And the unclean spirit, tearing him and crying out with a loud voice, went out of him. And they were all amazed...saying: What thing is this? What is this new doctrine?

... And there came a leper to him, beseeching him and kneeling down, said to him: If thou wilt thou canst make me clean. And Jesus, having compassion on him, stretched forth his hand and touching him saith to him: I will. Be thou made clean. And when he had spoken, immediately the leprosy departed from him: and he was made clean.

...And they came to him, bringing one sick of the palsy (paralysis), who was carried by four. And when they could not offer him unto him for the multitude, they uncovered the roof where he was: and opening it, they let down the bed wherein the man sick of the palsy lay. And when Jesus had seen their faith, he saith to the sick of the palsy: Son, thy sins are forgiven thee. And there were some of the scribes sitting there and thinking in their hearts: Why doth this man speak thus? He blasphemeth. Who can forgive sins, but God only? Which Jesus presently knowing in his spirit that they so thought within themselves, saith to them: Why think you these things in your hearts? Which is easier, to say to the sick of the palsy: Thy sins are forgiven thee; or to say: Arise, take up thy bed and walk? But that you may know that the Son of man hath power on earth to forgive sins (he saith to the sick of the palsy): I say to thee: Arise. Take up thy bed and go into thy house. And immediately he arose and, taking up his bed, went his way in the sight of all: so that all wondered and glorified God, saying: We never saw the like.

...And there arose a great storm of wind, and the waves beat into the ship, so that the ship was filled. And he was in the hinder part of the ship, sleeping upon a pillow; and they awake him, and say to him: Master, doth, it not concern thee that we perish? And rising up, he rebuked the wind, and said to the sea: Peace, be still. And the wind ceased: and there was made a great calm. And he said to them: Why are you fearful? have you not faith yet?

...And he commanded them that they should make them all sit down by companies upon the green grass. And they sat down in ranks, by hundreds and by fifties. And when he had taken the five loaves, and the two fishes: looking up to heaven, he blessed, and broke the loaves, and gave to his disciples to set before them: and the two fishes he divided among them all. And they all did eat and had their fill. And they took up the leavings, twelve full baskets of fragments, and of the fishes. And they that did eat, were five thousand men.

...And they came to Bethsaida: and they bring to him a blind man. And they besought him that he would touch him. And taking the blind man by the hand, he led him out of the town. And spitting upon his eyes, laying his hands on him, he asked him if he saw anything. And looking up, he said: I see men, as it were trees, walking. After that again he laid his hands upon his eyes: and he began to see and was restored, so that he saw all things clearly.

…And calling the multitude together with his disciples, he said to them: If any man will follow me, let him deny himself and take up his cross and follow me. For whosoever will save his life shall lose it: and whosoever shall lose his life for my sake and the gospel shall save it. For what shall it profit a man, if he gain the whole world and suffer the loss of his soul?

The Death & Resurrection of Jesus

…And they came to Jerusalem. And when he was entered into the temple, he began to cast out them that sold and bought in the temple: and overthrew the tables of the moneychangers and the chairs of them that sold doves. And he suffered not that any man should carry a vessel through the temple. And he taught, saying to them: Is it not written: My house shall be called the house of prayer to all nations, but you have made it a den of thieves. Which when the chief priests and the scribes had heard, they sought how they might destroy him. For they feared him, because the whole multitude was in admiration at his doctrine.

…And they brought Jesus to the high priest…the chief priests and all the council sought for evidence against Jesus, that they might put him to death: and found none. For many bore false witness against him: and their evidences were not agreeing. And some rising up, bore false witness against him, saying: We heard him say, I Will destroy this temple made with hands and within three days I will build another not made with hands. And their witness did not agree. And the high priest rising up in the midst, asked Jesus, saying: Answerest thou nothing to the things that are laid to thy charge by these men? But he held his peace and answered nothing. Again the high priest asked him and said to him: Art thou the Christ, the Son of the Blessed God? And Jesus said to him: I am. And you shall see the Son of man sitting on the right hand of the power of God and coming with the clouds of heaven. Then the high priest rending his garments, saith: What need we any further witnesses? You have heard the blasphemy. What think you? Who all condemned him to be guilty of death?

...And the soldiers led him away into the court of the palace: and they called together the whole band. And they clothed him with purple: and, platting a crown of thorns, they put it upon him. And they began to salute him: Hail, king of the Jews. And they struck his head with a reed: and they did spit on him. And bowing their knees, they adored him. And after they had mocked him, they took off the purple from him and put his own garments on him: and they led him out to crucify him.

...And when the sixth hour was come, there was darkness over the whole earth until the ninth hour. And at the ninth hour, Jesus cried out with a loud voice, saying: Eloi, Eloi, lamma sabacthani? Which is, being interpreted: My God, My God, why hast thou forsaken me? ...And Jesus, having cried out with a loud voice, gave up the ghost. And the veil of the temple was rent in two, from the top to the bottom. And the centurion who stood over against him, seeing that crying out in this manner he had given up the ghost. said: Indeed this man was the son of God.

...And Joseph, buying fine linen and taking him down, wrapped him up in the fine linen and laid him in a sepulcher which was hewed out of a rock. And he rolled a stone to the door of the sepulcher. And Mary Magdalen and Mary the mother of Joseph, beheld where he was laid.

...And when the sabbath was past, Mary Magdalen and Mary the mother of James and Salome bought sweet spices, that coming, they might anoint Jesus. And very early in the morning, the first day of the week, they come to the sepulcher, the sun being now risen. And they said one to another: Who shall roll us back the stone from the door of the sepulcher? And looking, they saw the stone rolled back. For it was very great. And entering into the sepulcher, they saw a young man sitting on the right side, clothed with a white robe: and they were astonished. Who saith to them: Be not affrighted. you seek Jesus of Nazareth, who was crucified. He is risen: he is not here.

...And the Lord Jesus, after he had spoken to them (his apostles), was taken up into heaven and sitteth on the right hand of God. But they going forth preached everywhere: the Lord working withal, and confirming the word with signs that followed.

The Word of God
(Excerpts from the books of *John & Mark*)

***

Since the Beginning

In the beginning was the Word: and the Word was with God: and the Word was God. The same was in the beginning with God. All things were made by him: and without him was made nothing that was made. In him was life: and the life was the light of men. And the light shineth in darkness: and the darkness did not comprehend it.

***

Light of the World

For God so loved the world, as to give his only begotten Son: that whosoever believeth in him may not perish, but may have life everlasting. For God sent not his Son into the world, to judge the world: but that the world may be saved by him. He that believeth in him is not judged. But he that doth not believe is already judged: because he believeth not in the name of the only begotten Son of God. And this is the judgment: Because the light is come into the world and men loved darkness rather than the light: for their works were evil. For everyone that doth evil hateth the light and cometh not to the light, that his works may not be reproved. But he that doth truth cometh to the light, that his works may be made manifest: because they are done in God.

***

Source: *Douay-Rheims Bible* (DRB) with Bishop Challoner revision, 1752.

The Way to God's Kingdom

Thomas saith to him: Lord, we know not whither thou goest. And how can we know the way? Jesus saith to him: I am the way, and the truth, and the life. No man cometh to the Father, but by me.

If you had known me, you would without doubt have known my Father also: and from henceforth you shall know him. And you have seen him.

***

The Tree of Life: Commandment of Love

I am the true vine: and my Father is the husbandman (farmer). Every branch in me that beareth not fruit, he will take away: and everyone that beareth fruit, he will purge it, that it may bring forth more fruit. Now you are clean, by reason of the word which I have spoken to you. Abide in me: and I in you. As the branch cannot bear fruit of itself, unless it abide in the vine, so neither can you, unless you abide in me. I am the vine: you the branches. He that abideth in me, and I in him, the same beareth much fruit: for without me you can do nothing. If anyone abide not in me, he shall be cast forth as a branch and shall wither: and they shall gather him up and cast him into the fire: and he burneth. If you abide in me and my words abide in you, you shall ask whatever you will: and it shall be done unto you. In this is my Father glorified: that you bring forth very much fruit and become my disciples. As the Father hath loved me, I also have loved you. Abide in my love. If you keep my commandments, you shall abide in my love: as I also have kept my Father's commandments and do abide in his love. These things I have spoken to you, that my joy may be in you, and your joy may be filled.

This is my commandment, that you love one another, as I have loved you.

Greater love than this no man hath, that a man lay down his

life for his friends. You are my friends, if you do the things that I command you. I will not now call you servants: for the servant knoweth not what his lord doth. But I have called you friends. because all things, whatsoever I have heard of my Father, I have made known to you. You have not chosen me: but I have chosen you; and have appointed you, that you should go and should bring forth fruit; and your fruit should remain: that whatsoever you shall ask of the Father in my name, he may give it you. These things I command you, that you love one another.

***

The Greatest Commandment

And there came one of the scribes that had heard them reasoning together, and seeing that he had answered them well, asked him which was the first commandment of all. And Jesus answered him: The first commandment of all is, Hear, O Israel: the Lord thy God is one God. And thou shalt love the Lord thy God with thy whole heart and with thy whole soul and with thy whole mind and with thy whole strength. This is the first commandment. And the second is like to it: Thou shalt love thy neighbor as thyself. There is no other commandment greater than these.

The Kingdom of God
(Parables & excerpts from the books of *Matthew* & *Luke)*

***

Why Parables?

And when a very great multitude was gathered together and hastened out of the cities, unto him, he spoke by a parable. The sower went out to sow his seed. And as he sowed, some fell by the wayside. And it was trodden down: and the fowls of the air devoured it. And other some fell upon a rock. And as soon as it was sprung up, it withered away, because it had no moisture. And other some fell among thorns. And the thorns growing up with it, choked it. And other some fell upon good ground and, being sprung up, yielded fruit a hundredfold. Saying these things, he cried out: He that hath ears to hear, let him hear.

And his disciples asked him what this parable might be. To whom he said: To you it is given to know the mystery of the kingdom of God; but to the rest in parables, that seeing they may not see and hearing may not understand.

Now the parable is this: The seed is the word of God. And they by the wayside are they that hear: then the devil cometh and taketh the word out of their heart, lest believing they should be saved. Now they upon the rock are they who when they hear receive the word with joy: and these have no roots: for they believe for a while and in time of temptation they fall away. And that which fell among thorns are they who have heard and, going their way, are choked with the cares and riches and pleasures of this life and yield no fruit. But that on the good ground are they who in a good and perfect heart, hearing the word, keep it and bring forth fruit in patience.

***

Source: *Douay-Rheims Bible* (DRB) with Bishop Challoner revision, 1752.

The Parable of the Mustard Seed

The kingdom of heaven is like to a grain of mustard seed, which a man took and sowed in his field. Which is the least indeed of all seeds; but when it is grown up, it is greater than all herbs, and becometh a tree, so that the birds of the air come, and dwell in the branches thereof.

***

The Parable of The Prodigal Son

A certain man had two sons. And the younger of them said to his father: Father, give me the portion of substance that falleth to me. And he divided unto them his substance. And not many days after, the younger son, gathering all together, went abroad into a far country: and there wasted his substance, living riotously. And after he had spent all, there came a mighty famine in that country: and he began to be in want. And he went and cleaved to one of the citizens of that country. And he sent him into his farm to feed swine. And he would fain have filled his belly with the husks the swine did eat: and no man gave unto him. And returning to himself, he said: How many hired servants in my father's house abound with bread, and I here perish with hunger! I will arise and will go to my father and say to him: Father, I have sinned against heaven and before thee. I am not worthy to be called thy son: make me as one of thy hired servants. And rising up, he came to his father. And when he was yet a great way off, his father saw him and was moved with compassion and running to him fell upon his neck and kissed him. And the son said to him: Father: I have sinned against heaven and before thee I am not now worthy to be called thy son. And the father said to his servants: Bring forth quickly the first robe and put it on him: and put a ring on his hand and shoes on his feet. And bring hither the fatted calf and kill it: and let us eat and make merry: Because this my son was dead and is come to life again, was lost and is found. And they began to be merry.

Now his elder son was in the field and when he came and drew nigh to the house, he heard music and dancing. And he called one of the servants and asked what these things meant. And he said to him: Thy brother is come and thy father hath killed the fatted calf, because he hath received him safe. And he was angry and would not go in. His father therefore coming out began to entreat him. And he answering, said to his father: Behold, for so many years do I serve thee and I have never transgressed thy commandment: and yet thou hast never given me a kid to make merry with my friends. But as soon as this thy son is come, who hath devoured his substance with harlots, thou hast killed for him the fatted calf. But he said to him: Son, thou art always with me; and all I have is thine. But it was fit that we should make merry and be glad: for this thy brother was dead and is come to life again; he was lost and is found.

***

The Parable of Hidden Treasure

The kingdom of heaven is like unto a treasure hidden in a field. Which a man having found, hid it, and for joy thereof goeth, and selleth all that he hath, and buyeth that field.

***

Coming of the Kingdom

And being asked by the Pharisees when the kingdom of God should come, he answered them and said: The kingdom of God cometh not with observation. Neither shall they say: Behold here or behold there. For lo, the kingdom of God is within you.

The Sermon on the Mount
(From the book of *Matthew,* Ch. 5-7*)*

***

And seeing the multitudes, he went up into a mountain, and when he was set down, his disciples came unto him. And opening his mouth he taught them, saying:

Be Glad: The Beatitudes
Blessed are the poor in spirit: for theirs is the kingdom of heaven.
Blessed are the meek: for they shall possess the land.
Blessed are they that mourn: for they shall be comforted.
Blessed are they that hunger and thirst after justice: for they shall have their fill.
Blessed are the merciful: for they shall obtain mercy.
Blessed are the clean of heart: they shall see God.
Blessed are the peacemakers: for they shall be called the children of God.
Blessed are they that suffer persecution for justice' sake: for theirs is the kingdom of heaven.
Blessed are ye when they shall revile you, and persecute you, and speak all that is evil against you, untruly, for my sake: Be glad and rejoice for your reward is very great in heaven. For so they persecuted the prophets that were before you.

Shine Your Light for Others
You are the salt of the earth. But if the salt lose its savor, wherewith shall it be salted? It is good for nothing anymore but to be cast out, and to be trodden on by men.
You are the light of the world. A city seated on a mountain cannot be hid. Neither do men light a candle and put it under a bushel, but upon a candlestick, that it may shine to all that are in

---

Source: *Douay-Rheims Bible* (DRB) with Bishop Challoner revision, 1752.

the house. So let your light shine before men, that they may see your good works, and glorify your Father who is in heaven.

Fulfill the Law of Moses

Do not think that I am come to destroy the law, or the prophets. I am not come to destroy, but to fulfil. For amen I say unto you, till heaven and earth pass, one jot, or one tittle shall not pass of the law, till all be fulfilled. He therefore that shall break one of these least commandments and shall so teach men shall be called the least in the kingdom of heaven. But he that shall do and teach, he shall be called great in the kingdom of heaven.

For I tell you, that unless your justice abounds more than that of the scribes and Pharisees, you shall not enter into the kingdom of heaven.

Let go of Anger

You have heard that it was said to them of old: Thou shalt not kill. And whosoever shall kill, shall be in danger of the judgment. But I say to you, that whosoever is angry with his brother, shall be in danger of the judgment. And whosoever shall say to his brother, Raca, shall be in danger of the council. And whosoever shall say, Thou fool, shall be in danger of hell fire. If therefore thou offer thy gift at the altar, and there thou remember that thy brother hath anything against thee; Leave there thy offering before the altar, and go first to be reconciled to thy brother, and then coming thou shalt offer thy gift. Be at agreement with thy adversary betimes, whilst thou art in the way with him: lest perhaps the adversary deliver thee to the judge, and the judge deliver thee to the officer, and thou be cast into prison. Amen I say to thee, thou shalt not go out from thence till thou repay the last farthing.

Have Purity of Heart

You have heard that it was said to them of old: Thou shalt not commit adultery. But I say to you, that whosoever shall look on a woman to lust after her, hath already committed adultery with her in his heart. And if thy right eye scandalizes thee, pluck it out and cast it from thee. For it is expedient for thee that one of thy members should perish, rather than thy whole body be cast into hell. And if thy right hand scandalizes thee, cut it off, and cast it from thee: for it is expedient for thee that one of thy members should perish, rather than that thy whole body go into hell.

Be Responsible to Your Partner

And it hath been said, whosoever shall put away his wife, let him give her a bill of divorce. But I say to you, that whosoever shall put away his wife, excepting the cause of fornication, maketh her to commit adultery: and he that shall marry her that is put away, committeth adultery.

Have Integrity

Again, you have heard that it was said to them of old, thou shalt not forswear thyself: but thou shalt perform thy oaths to the Lord. But I say to you not to swear at all, neither by heaven for it is the throne of God: Nor by the earth, for it is his footstool: nor by Jerusalem, for it is the city of the great king: Neither shalt thou swear by thy head, because thou canst not make one hair white or black. But let your speech be yea, yea: no, no: and that which is over and above these, is of evil.

Love Your Enemies

You have heard that it hath been said: An eye for an eye, and a tooth for a tooth. But I say to you not to resist evil: but if one strike thee on thy right cheek, turn to him also the other: And if a man will contend with thee in judgment, and take away thy coat, let go thy cloak also unto him. And whosoever will force thee one mile, go with him other two. Give to him that asketh of thee, and from him that would borrow of thee turn not away.

You have heard that it hath been said, Thou shalt love thy neighbour, and hate thy enemy. But I say to you, Love your enemies: do good to them that hate you: and pray for them that persecute and calumniate you: That you may be the children of your Father who is in heaven, who maketh his sun to rise upon the good, and bad, and raineth upon the just and the unjust. For if you love them that love you, what reward shall you have? do not even the publicans this? And if you salute your brethren only, what do you more? do not also the heathens this? Be you therefore perfect, as also your heavenly Father is perfect.

Give Selflessly

Take heed that you do not do your justice before men, to be seen by them: otherwise you shall not have a reward of your Father who is in heaven.

Therefore, when thou dost an alms-deed, sound not a trumpet before thee, as the hypocrites do in the synagogues and in the streets, that they may be honoured by men. Amen I say to you, they have received their reward. But when thou dost alms, let not thy left hand know what thy right hand doth. That thy alms may be in secret, and thy Father who seeth in secret will repay thee.

Say the Lord's Prayer

And when ye pray, you shall not be as the hypocrites, that love to stand and pray in the synagogues and corners of the streets, that they may be seen by men: Amen I say to you, they have received their reward. But thou when thou shalt pray, enter into thy chamber, and having shut the door, pray to thy Father in secret, and thy father who seeth in secret will repay thee.

And when you are praying, speak not much, as the heathens. For they think that in their much speaking they may be heard. Be not you therefore like to them for your Father knoweth what is needful for you, before you ask him.

Thus, therefore shall you pray: Our Father who art in heaven, hallowed be thy name.

Thy kingdom come. Thy will be done on earth as it is in heaven.

Give us this day our supersubstantial bread. And forgive us our debts, as we also forgive our debtors. And lead us not into temptation. But deliver us from evil. Amen. For if you will forgive men their offences, your heavenly Father will forgive you also your offences. But if you will not forgive men, neither will your Father forgive you your offences.

Practice with Humility

And when you fast, be not as the hypocrites, sad. For they disfigure their faces, that they may appear unto men to fast. Amen I say to you, they have received their reward. But thou, when thou fastest anoint thy head, and wash thy face; That thou appear not to men to fast, but to thy Father who is in secret: and thy Father who seeth in secret, will repay thee.

Seek Treasures in Heaven

Lay not up to yourselves treasures on earth: where the rust, and moth consume, and where thieves break through, and steal. But lay up to yourselves treasures in heaven: where neither the rust nor moth doth consume, and where thieves do not break through, nor steal. For where thy treasure is, there is thy heart also.

Focus Your Life on the Light

The light of thy body is thy eye. If thy eye be single, thy whole body shall be lightsome. But if thy eye be evil thy whole body shall be darksome. If then the light that is in thee, be darkness: the darkness itself how great shall it be!

No man can serve two masters. For either he will hate the one and love the other: or he will sustain the one, and despise the other. You cannot serve God and mammon.

Let Go of Worry

Therefore I say to you, be worry for your life, what you shall eat, nor for your body, what you shall put on. Is not the life more than the meat: and the body more than the raiment? Behold the birds of the air, for they neither sow, nor do they reap, nor gather into barns: and your heavenly Father feedeth them. Are not you of much more value than they? And which of you by taking thought, can add to his stature one cubit? And for raiment why do you worry? Consider the lilies of the field, how they grow: they labor not, neither do they spin. But I say to you, that not even Solomon in all his glory was arrayed as one of these. And if the grass of the field, which is today, and tomorrow is cast into the oven, God doth so clothe: how much more you, O ye of little faith? Be not solicitous therefore, saying: What shall we eat: or what shall we drink, or wherewith shall we be clothed? For after all these things do the heathens seek. For your Father knoweth that you have need of all these things. Seek ye therefore first the kingdom of God, and his justice, and all these things shall be added unto you.

Be not therefore worrisome for tomorrow; for tomorrow will worry for itself. Enough exists for you to contend with today.

Let Go of Judgment

Judge not, that you may not be judged. For with what judgment you judge, you shall be judged: and with what measure you mete, it shall be measured to you again. And why seest thou the mote that is in thy brother's eye; and seest not the beam that is in thy own eye? Or how sayest thou to thy brother: Let me cast the mote out of thy eye; and behold a beam is in thy own eye? Thou hypocrite, cast out first the beam out of thy own eye, and then shalt thou see to cast out the mote out of thy brother's eye.

Give not that which is holy to dogs; neither cast ye your pearls before swine, lest perhaps they trample them under their feet, and turning upon you, they tear you.

Ask, Seek, and Knock

Ask, and it shall be given you: seek, and you shall find: knock, and it shall be opened to you. For everyone that asketh, receiveth: and he that seeketh, findeth: and to him that knocketh, it shall be opened. Or what man is there among you, of whom if his son shall ask bread, will he reach him a stone? Or if he shall ask him a fish, will he reach him a serpent? If you then being evil, know how to give good gifts to your children: how much more will your Father who is in heaven, give good things to them that ask him?

Follow the Golden Rule

All things therefore whatsoever you would that men should do to you, do you also to them. For this is the law and the prophets.

Enter the Narrow Gate

Enter ye in at the narrow gate: for wide is the gate, and broad is the way that leadeth to destruction, and many there are who go in thereat. How narrow is the gate, and strait is the way that leadeth to life: and few there are that find it!

Eat of Good Fruit

Beware of false prophets, who come to you in the clothing of sheep, but inwardly they are ravening wolves. By their fruits you shall know them. Do men gather grapes of thorns, or figs of thistles? Even so every good tree bringeth forth good fruit, and the evil tree bringeth forth evil fruit. A good tree cannot bring forth evil fruit, neither can an evil tree bring forth good fruit. Every tree that bringeth not forth good fruit, shall be cut down, and shall be cast into the fire. Wherefore by their fruits you shall know them.

Follow God's Will to the Kingdom

Not everyone that saith to me, Lord, Lord, shall enter into the kingdom of heaven: but he that doth the will of my Father who is in heaven, he shall enter into the kingdom of heaven. Many will say to me in that day: Lord, Lord, have not we prophesied in thy name, and cast out devils in thy name, and done many miracles in thy name? And then will I profess unto them, I never knew you: depart from me, you that work iniquity.

Build Your Life on this Rock
Every one therefore that heareth these my words, and doth them, shall be likened to a wise man that built his house upon a rock, And the rain fell, and the floods came, and the winds blew, and they beat upon that house, and it fell not, for it was founded on a rock. And every one that heareth these my words and doth them not, shall be like a foolish man that built his house upon the sand, And the rain fell, and the floods came, and the winds blew, and they beat upon that house, and it fell, and great was the fall thereof.

The Authority of Jesus
And it came to pass when Jesus had fully ended these words, the people were in admiration at his doctrine. For he was teaching them as one having power, and not as the scribes and Pharisees.

The Nature of Faith
(Excerpts from the book of *Hebrews,* Ch. 11)

***

Now, faith is the substance of things to be hoped for, the evidence of things that appear not. For by this the ancients obtained a testimony.

By faith we understand that the world was framed by the word of God: that from invisible things visible things might be made.

***

But without faith it is impossible to please God. For he that cometh to God must believe that he is: and is a rewarder to them that seek him. By faith Noah, having received an answer concerning those things which as yet were not seen, moved with fear, framed the ark for the saving of his house: by the which he condemned the world and was instituted heir of the justice which is by faith.

***

By faith he that is called Abraham obeyed to go out into a place which he was to receive for an inheritance. And he went out, not knowing whither he went. By faith he abode in the land of promise, as in a strange country, dwelling in cottages, with Isaac and Jacob, the co-heirs of the same promise. For he looked for a city that hath foundations: whose builder and maker is God. By faith also Sara herself, being barren, received strength to conceive seed, even past the time of age: because she believed that he was faithful who had promised, For which cause there sprung even from one (and him as good as dead) as the stars of

---

Source: *Douay-Rheims Bible* (DRB) with Bishop Challoner revision, 1752.

heaven in multitude and as the sand which is by the sea shore innumerable.

All these died according to faith, not having received the promises but beholding them afar off and saluting them and confessing that they are pilgrims and strangers on the earth. For they that say these things do signify that they seek a country. And truly, if they had been mindful of that from whence they came out, they had doubtless, time to return. But now they desire a better, that is to say, a heavenly country. Therefore, God is not ashamed to be called their God: for he hath prepared for them a city.

***

By faith Abraham, when he was tried, offered Isaac: and he that had received the promises offered up his only begotten son, (To whom it was said: In Isaac shalt thy seed be called:) Accounting that God is able to raise up even from the dead. Whereupon also he received him for a parable.

***

By faith Moses, when he was born, was hid three months by his parents: because they saw he was a comely babe, and they feared not the king's edict. By faith Moses, when he was grown up, denied himself to be the son of Pharaoh's daughter: Rather choosing to be afflicted with the people of God than to have the pleasure of sin for a time: Esteeming the reproach of Christ greater riches than the treasure of the Egyptians. For he looked unto the reward. By faith he left Egypt, not fearing the fierceness of the king: for he endured, as seeing him that is invisible. By faith he celebrated the pasch and the shedding of the blood: that he who destroyed the firstborn might not touch them. By faith they passed through the Red Sea, as by dry land: which the Egyptians attempting, were swallowed up.

CHAPTER SEVEN

Islam

Remembering THE God

(Excerpts from *The Holy Qur'an*)

***

Surah Fatiha: The Opening

In the name of God, Most Gracious, Most Merciful.
Praise be to God, the Cherisher and Sustainer of the worlds;
Most Gracious, Most Merciful;
Master of the Day of Judgment.
Thee do we worship, and Thine aid we seek.
Show us the straight way,
The way of those on whom Thou hast bestowed Thy Grace,
those whose (portion) is not wrath, and who go not astray.

***

The Book

This is the Book; in it is guidance sure, without doubt, to those who fear God.

***

The One True God

If there were, in the heavens and the earth, other gods besides God, there would have been confusion in both! but glory to God, the Lord of the Throne: (High is He) above what they attribute to Him!

He cannot be questioned for His acts, but they will be questioned (for theirs).

Source: *The Holy Qur'an,* translated by Abdullah Yusuf Ali. Shaik Muhammed Ashraf Publishers, 1938.

Or have they taken for worship (other) gods besides him? Say, "Bring your convincing proof: this (the Qur'an) is the Message of those with me and the Message of those before me." But most of them know not the Truth, and so turn away.

Not an apostle did We send before thee without this inspiration sent by Us to him: that there is no god but I; therefore worship and serve Me.

***

Refocusing on God

The mutual rivalry for piling up (worldly gains) diverts you (from remembering God),

This is the true account: There is no god except God. And God, He is indeed the Exalted in Power, the Wise.
But if they turn back, God hath full knowledge of those who do mischief.
Say: "O People of the Book! come to common terms as between us and you: That we worship none but God. that we associate no partners with him; that we erect not, from among ourselves, Lords and patrons other than God." If then they turn back, say ye: "Bear witness that we (at least) are Muslims (bowing to God's Will).

"Those who believe, and whose hearts find satisfaction in the remembrance of God. for without doubt in the remembrance of God do hearts find satisfaction.

***

Mankind United

Mankind was one single nation, and God sent Messengers with glad tidings and warnings; and with them He sent the Book in truth, to judge between people in matters wherein they differed; but the People of the Book, after the clear Signs came to them, did not differ among themselves, except through selfish contumacy. God by His Grace Guided the believers to the Truth, concerning that wherein they differed. For God guided whom He will to a path that is straight.

O mankind! We created you from a single (pair) of a male and a female, and made you into nations and tribes, that ye may know each other (not that ye may despise (each other).

**

Following the Prophets of Judaism & Christianity

To those who believe in God and His apostles and make no distinction between any of the apostles, we shall soon give their (due) rewards: for God is Oft- forgiving, Most Merciful.

We have sent thee inspiration, as We sent it to Noah and the Messengers after him: we sent inspiration to Abraham, Isma'il, Isaac, Jacob and the Tribes, to Jesus, Job, Jonah, Aaron, and Solomon, and to David We gave the Psalms.
Of some apostles We have already told thee the story; of others We have not;- and to Moses God spoke direct;-

The same religion has He established for you as that which He enjoined on Noah - the which We have sent by inspiration to thee - and that which We enjoined on Abraham, Moses, and Jesus: Namely, that ye should remain steadfast in religion, and make no divisions therein: to those who worship other things than God, hard is the (way) to which thou callest them. God chooses to Himself those whom He pleases, and guides to Himself those who turn (to Him).
And they became divided only after Knowledge reached

them,- through selfish envy as between themselves. Had it not been for a Word that went forth before from thy Lord, (tending) to a Term appointed, the matter would have been settled between them: But truly those who have inherited the Book after them are in suspicious (disquieting) doubt concerning it.

Now then, for that (reason), call (them to the Faith), and stand steadfast as thou art commanded, nor follow thou their vain desires; but say: "I believe in the Book which God has sent down; and I am commanded to judge justly between you. God is our Lord and your Lord: for us (is the responsibility for) our deeds, and for you for your deeds. There is no contention between us and you. God will bring us together, and to Him is (our) Final Goal.

When Jesus came with Clear Signs, he said: "Now have I come to you with Wisdom, and in order to make clear to you some of the (points) on which ye dispute: therefore fear God and obey me.

"For God, He is my Lord and your Lord: so worship ye Him: this is a Straight Way."

But sects from among themselves fell into disagreement: then woe to the wrong-doers, from the Penalty of a Grievous Day!

***

The Fall of Adam from The Garden

"O Adam! dwell thou and thy wife in the Garden and enjoy (its good things) as ye wish: but approach not this tree, or ye run into harm and transgression."

Then began Satan to whisper suggestions to them, bringing openly before their minds all their shame that was hidden from them (before): he said: "Your Lord only forbade you this tree, lest ye should become angels or such beings as live forever."

And he swore to them both, that he was their sincere

adviser.

So by deceit he brought about their fall: when they tasted of the tree, their shame became manifest to them, and they began to sew together the leaves of the garden over their bodies. And their Lord called unto them: "Did I not forbid you that tree, and tell you that Satan was an avowed enemy unto you?"

They said: "Our Lord! We have wronged our own souls: If thou forgive us not and bestow not upon us Thy Mercy, we shall certainly be lost."

((God)) said: "Get ye down. With enmity between yourselves. On earth will be your dwelling-place and your means of livelihood,- for a time."

He said: "Therein shall ye live, and therein shall ye die; but from it shall ye be taken out (at last)."

O ye Children of Adam! We have bestowed raiment upon you to cover your shame, as well as to be an adornment to you. But the raiment of righteousness,- that is the best. Such are among the Signs of God, that they may receive admonition!

O ye Children of Adam! Let not Satan seduce you, in the same manner as He got your parents out of the Garden, stripping them of their raiment, to expose their shame: for he and his tribe watch you from a position where ye cannot see them: We made the evil ones friends (only) to those without faith.

***

Judgment Day: Hell or Garden

No just estimate have they made of God, such as is due to Him: On the Day of Judgment the whole of the earth will be but His handful, and the heavens will be rolled up in His right hand: Glory to Him! High is He above the Partners they attribute to Him!

The Trumpet will (just) be sounded, when all that are in the heavens and on earth will swoon, except such as it will please

God (to exempt). Then will a second one be sounded, when, behold, they will be standing and looking on!

And the Earth will shine with the Glory of its Lord: the Record (of Deeds) will be placed (open); the prophets and the witnesses will be brought forward and a just decision pronounced between them; and they will not be wronged (in the least).

And to every soul will be paid in full (the fruit) of its Deeds; and ((God)) knoweth best all that they do.

The Unbelievers will be led to Hell in crowd: until, when they arrive, there, its gates will be opened. And its keepers will say, "Did not apostles come to you from among yourselves, rehearsing to you the Signs of your Lord, and warning you of the Meeting of This Day of yours?" The answer will be: "True: but the Decree of Punishment has been proved true against the Unbelievers!"

(To them) will be said: "Enter ye the gates of Hell, to dwell therein: and evil is (this) Abode of the Arrogant!"

And those who feared their Lord will be led to the Garden in crowds: until behold, they arrive there; its gates will be opened; and its keepers will say: "Peace be upon you! well have ye done! enter ye here, to dwell therein."

Enter ye the Garden, ye and your wives, in (beauty and) rejoicing.

To them will be passed round, dishes and goblets of gold: there will be there all that the souls could desire, all that their ayes could delight in: and ye shall abide therein (for eye).

Such will be the Garden of which ye are made heirs for your (good) deeds (in life).

Ye shall have therein abundance of fruit, from which ye shall have satisfaction.

The sinners will be in the Punishment of Hell, to dwell therein (for aye):

Nowise will the (Punishment) be lightened for them, and in despair will they be there overwhelmed.

Nowise shall We be unjust to them: but it is they who have been unjust themselves.

They will cry: "O Malik! would that thy Lord put an end to us!" He will say, "Nay, but ye shall abide!"

Verily We have brought the Truth to you: but most of you have a hatred for Truth.

***

What Kind of Person Should You Be?

It is not righteousness that ye turn your faces Towards east or West; but it is righteousness- to believe in God and the Last Day, and the Angels, and the Book, and the Messengers; to spend of your substance, out of love for Him, for your kin, for orphans, for the needy, for the wayfarer, for those who ask, and for the ransom of slaves; to be steadfast in prayer, and practice regular charity; to fulfil the contracts which ye have made; and to be firm and patient, in pain (or suffering) and adversity, and throughout all periods of panic. Such are the people of truth,

Be quick in the race for forgiveness from your Lord, and for a Garden whose width is that (of the whole) of the heavens and of the earth, prepared for the righteous,-

Those who spend (freely), whether in prosperity, or in adversity; who restrain anger, and pardon (all) men;- for God loves those who do good;-

... We have made some of you as a trial for others: will ye have patience?

And let me not be in disgrace on the Day when (men) will be raised up;-

The Day whereon neither wealth nor sons will avail,

But only he (will prosper) that brings to God a sound heart.

151

God, The Beloved
(Selected poetry by Rumi)

***

The Music of Love

Hail to thee, then, O LOVE, sweet madness!
Thou who healest all our infirmities!
Who art the Physician of our pride and self-conceit!
Who art our Plato and our Galen!
Love exalts our earthly bodies to heaven,
And makes the very hills to dance with joy!
O lover, 'twas Love that gave life to Mount Sinai,
When "it quaked, and Moses fell down in a swoon."
Did my Beloved only touch me with His lips,
I too, like a flute, would burst out into melody.

***

When the Rose has Faded

When the rose has faded and the garden is withered,
The song of the nightingale is no longer to be heard.
The BELOVED is all in all, the lover only veils Him;
The BELOVED is all that lives, the lover a dead thing.
When the lover feels no longer LOVE'S quickening,
He becomes like a bird who has lost its wings. Alas!
How can I retain my senses about me,
When the BELOVED shows not the Light of His countenance?

Source: *Jalálu'd-dín Rúmí*, by F. Hadland Davis. Published by John Murray, Albemarle Street, W., 1920.

Thou Art the Soul of the World

Eternal Life, methinks, is the time of Union,
Because Time, for me, hath no place There.
Life is the vessels, Union the clear draught in them;
Without Thee what does the pain of the vessels avail me?
I had twenty thousand desires ere this;
In passion for Him not even (care of) my safety remained.
By the help of His grace I am become safe, because
The unseen King saith to me, "Thou art the soul of the world."
"Behold the Water of the Waters"!
When you have accepted the Light, O beloved,
When you behold what is veiled without a veil,
Like a star you will walk upon the heavens.

***

The Voice of Love

Every moment the voice of Love is coming from left and right.
We are bound for heaven: who has a mind to sight-seeing?
We have been in heaven, we have been friends of the angels;
Thither, Sire, let us return, for that is our country.

The Sea of Love

Mankind, like waterfowl, are sprung from the sea—the Sea of
    Soul;
Risen from that Sea, why should the bird make here his home?
Nay, we are pearls in that Sea, therein we all abide;
Else, why does wave follow wave from the Sea of Soul?
'Tis the time of Union's attainment, 'tis the time of Eternity's
    beauty,
'Tis the time of favour and largesse, 'tis the Ocean of perfect
    purity.
The billow of largesse hath appeared, the thunder of the Sea
    hath arrived,
The morn of blessedness hath dawned. Morn? No, 'tis the Light
    of God.

***

The Beauty of the Beloved

O Beloved, spiritual beauty is very fair and glorious,
But Thine own beauty and loveliness is another thing.
O Thou who art years describing Spirit,
Show one quality that is equal to His Essence.
Light waxes in the eye at the imagination of Him,
But in presence of His Union it is dimmed.
I stand open-mouthed in veneration of that beauty:
"God is most great" is on my heart's lips every moment.
The heart hath gotten an eye constant in desire of Thee.
O how that desire feeds heart and eye!
'Tis slave-caressing Thy Love has practiced;
Else, where is the heart worthy of that Love?
Every heart that has slept one night in Thy air
Is like radiant day.

154

God Only

"None but God has contemplated the beauty of God."
This eye and that lamp are two lights, each individual,
When they came together, no one distinguished them.

***

The Finding of the Beloved

I was on that day when the Names were not,
Nor any sign of existence endowed with name,
By me Names and Named were brought to view
On the day when there was not "I" and "We,"
For a sign, the tip of the Beloved's curl became a center of
    revelation;
As yet the tip of that curl was not.
Cross and Christians, from end to end,
I surveyed; He was not on the Cross.
I went to the idol-temple, to the ancient pagoda;
No trace was visible there.
I went to the mountains of Herāt and Candahār;
I looked; He was not in that hill-and-dale.

I gazed into my own heart;
There I saw Him; He was nowhere else.

Earthly Love and the Love Divine

'Twere better that the spirit which wears not true Love as a
    garment
Had not been: its being is but shame.

Without the dealing of Love there is no entrance to the Beloved.

'Tis Love and the Lover that live to all Eternity;
Set not thy heart on aught else; 'tis only borrowed,
How long wilt thou embrace a dead beloved?
Embrace the Soul which is embraced by nothing.
What was born of spring dies in autumn,
Love's rose-plot hath no aiding from the early spring.

***

The Flame of Love

How long wilt thou dwell on words and superficialities?
A burning heart is what I want; consort with burning!
Kindle in thy heart the flame of Love,
And burn up utterly thoughts and fine expressions.
O Moses! the lovers of fair rites are one class,
They whose hearts and souls burn with Love another.

The Love of the Beloved

No lover ever seeks union with his beloved,
But his beloved is also seeking union with him.
But the lover's love makes his body lean,
While the Beloved's love makes her fair and lusty.
When in this heart the lightning spark of love arises,
Be sure this Love is reciprocated in that heart.
When the Love of God arises in thy heart,
Without doubt God also feels love for thee.

***

This is Love

This is Love: to fly heavenward,
To rend, every instant, a hundred veils.
The first moment, to renounce Life:
The last step, to feel without feet.
To regard this world as invisible,
Not to see what appears to one's self.
"O heart," I said, "may it bless thee
To have entered the circle of lovers,
To look beyond the range of the eye,
To penetrate the windings of the bosom!
Whence did this breath come to thee, O my soul,
Whence this throbbing, O my heart?"

Sufi Stories
(Various Sufi wisdom tales)

***

Moths and the Flame (Farid ud-Din-Attar)

At night the moths assembled, tortured by desire to be one with the candle. "We must find one who can share the knowledge that we long for."

A single moth flew to the palace and saw the light of the candle within. She shared her experience with the others. "She has no real knowledge to share," said the wisest among them.

Another, flew to the candle, venturing closer to the light, touching the flame with her wings. She also shared her experience, explaining what it is like to be one with the candle. "She too has no real knowledge to share," said the wisest among them.

The third moth had risen and hurled herself into the candle's flame. Immersed wholly in its embrace, she transformed into shining redness, as like the flame. The wise moth saw the candle had identified with the moth and shared with the moth its light. "Only this moth knows. No others do."

Source: original adaptation by the author.

Nasrudin & The Lost Key

One cool night, a stranger was walking along a lit path when he found the Mulla Nasrudin on hands and knees. "What are you doing?" asked the stranger.

"I'm searching for the key to my home," replied the Mulla.

"Oh, how awful," replied the stranger. "Let me help you find it."

The stranger dropped to his hands and knees and began searching too. After a little while, when perspiration began dripping from his brow, the stranger asked, "where exactly did you last see it?"

The Mulla turned back and gestured towards his house, several meters away. "Somewhere inside there."

The stranger was perplexed and agitated. "What?! So why are you searching out here on the path."

The Mulla replied, "there is better lighting out here than in there."

Nasrudin's Sermon

The townspeople were mischievous and decided to have fun at the Mulla Nasrudin's expense. Since he was known to be a sort of spiritual man they proclaimed, "Let us hear him preach and expose him as a fraud!"

The Mulla accepted their invitation to preach at their mosque. On Friday, he began his first sermon with a question. "Peace be unto you. Do you possess knowledge of what I will teach you?"

The townspeople looked at each other, then proclaimed, "No! We do not possess such knowledge."

Disgusted, the Mulla replied, "If you do not know, I cannot speak to you." And to a stunned crowd, he abruptly returned home.

The following week, the townspeople were undeterred and asked the Mulla to preach again.

For his second sermon, the Mulla began with the same question. "Peace be unto you. Do you possess knowledge of what I will teach you?"

Chuckling, the townspeople looked at each other, then proclaimed, "Yes! We do possess such knowledge."

The Mulla replied, "Fine then. Since you already have the knowledge, I have nothing new to give you." And to a confused crowd, he abruptly returned home.

At last, the townspeople were convinced they knew how to fool the Mulla. So, they invited him a third time.

The Mulla began his sermon as before. "Do you possess knowledge of what I will teach?"

After conferring the night before, the crowd in unison proclaimed, "Half of us have it and half of us do not!"

The Mulla replied gleefully, "How wonderful! The half that knows shall teach the half that doesn't."

And with a smile of satisfaction, the Mulla abruptly returned home.

Nasrudin & The Truth

There once was a land full of injustice due to deceit. In the attempt to purge this kingdom of liars and frauds, the king passed a new law. "Only foreigners who tell the truth of their visit shall be spared. All those caught in a lie shall be put to death."

Upon hearing this news, the Mulla Nasrudin mounted his donkey and journeyed to visit the kingdom.

"What is the purpose of your visit?" asked the guardians of the gate. "Be warned, you shall be put to death if you fail to provide the truth."

"Perfect!" said the Mulla joyfully. "The purpose of my visit...I will be put to death."

"That cannot be!" proclaimed one guardian.

"Foolish Mulla. Nobody comes here to be put to death. You must be lying!" proclaimed the other.

With disgust, the Mulla replied, "You think the truth out here is the same as the truth inside the kingdom?"

"What do you mean?" asked the guardians. "Truth is truth."

"In that case, put me to death!" exclaimed the Mulla.

As one guardian was about to strike the Mulla down, the other intervened, as his eyes suddenly saw the irony of such action. "We can't put him to death, for his death shall then be unjust since he would have given us the truth."

The other guardian replied, "Wait! But if we let him go, he would be a liar, since he will not be put to death."

While the guardians stood frozen and perplexed, the Mulla signaled to his donkey to continue into the kingdom.

Once through the gates, without a turn of his head, the Mulla muttered,

"So, who is the fool now..."

The Heifer

(Excerpts from Sura 2 from *The Holy Qur'an*)

***

This is the Book; in it is guidance sure, without doubt, to those who fear God.

Who believe in the Unseen, are steadfast in prayer, and spend out of what We have provided for them;

And who believe in the Revelation sent to thee, and sent before thy time, and (in their hearts) have the assurance of the Hereafter.

They are on (true) guidance, from their Lord, and it is these who will prosper.

As to those who reject Faith, it is the same to them whether thou warn them or do not warn them; they will not believe.

God hath set a seal on their hearts and on their hearing, and on their eyes is a veil; great is the penalty they (incur).

Of the people there are some who say: "We believe in God and the Last Day;" but they do not (really) believe.

Fain would they deceive God and those who believe, but they only deceive themselves, and realize (it) not!

In their hearts is a disease; and God has increased their disease: And grievous is the penalty they (incur), because they are false (to themselves).

When it is said to them: "Make not mischief on the earth," they say: "Why, we only Want to make peace!"

Of a surety, they are the ones who make mischief, but they realize (it) not.

When it is said to them: "Believe as the others believe:" They say: "Shall we believe as the fools believe?" Nay, of a surety they are the fools, but they do not know.

When they meet those who believe, they say: "We believe;"

Source: *The Holy Qur'an,* translated by Abdullah Yusuf Ali. Shaik Muhammed Ashraf Publishers, 1938.

but when they are alone with their evil ones, they say: "We are really with you: We (were) only jesting."

God will throw back their mockery on them, and give them rope in their trespasses; so they will wander like blind ones (To and fro).

These are they who have bartered Guidance for error: But their traffic is profitless, and they have lost true direction,

Their similitude is that of a man who kindled a fire; when it lighted all around him, God took away their light and left them in utter darkness. So they could not see.

Deaf, dumb, and blind, they will not return (to the path).

Or (another similitude) is that of a rain-laden cloud from the sky: In it are zones of darkness, and thunder and lightning: They press their fingers in their ears to keep out the stunning thunder-clap, the while they are in terror of death. But God is ever round the rejecters of Faith!

The lightning all but snatches away their sight; every time the light (Helps) them, they walk therein, and when the darkness grows on them, they stand still. And if God willed, He could take away their faculty of hearing and seeing; for God hath power over all things.

O ye people! Adore your Guardian-Lord, who created you and those who came before you, that ye may have the chance to learn righteousness.

Who has made the earth your couch, and the heavens your canopy; and sent down rain from the heavens; and brought forth therewith Fruits for your sustenance; then set not up rivals unto God when ye know (the truth)?

And if ye are in doubt as to what We have revealed from time to time to Our servant, then produce a Sura like thereunto; and call your witnesses or helpers (If there are any) besides God, if your (doubts) are true.

But if ye cannot- and of a surety ye cannot- then fear the Fire whose fuel is men and stones,- which is prepared for those who reject Faith.

But give glad tidings to those who believe and work

righteousness, that their portion is Gardens, beneath which rivers flow. Every time they are fed with fruits therefrom, they say: "Why, this is what we were fed with before," for they are given things in similitude; and they have therein companions pure (and holy); and they abide therein (forever).

God disdains not to use the similitude of things, lowest as well as highest. Those who believe know that it is truth from their Lord; but those who reject Faith say: "What means God by this similitude?" By it He causes many to stray, and many He leads into the right path; but He causes not to stray, except those who forsake (the path), -

Those who break God's Covenant after it is ratified, and who sunder what God Has ordered to be joined and do mischief on earth: These cause loss (only) to themselves.

How can ye reject the faith in God.- seeing that ye were without life, and He gave you life; then will He cause you to die, and will again bring you to life; and again to Him will ye return.

It is He Who hath created for you all things that are on earth; Moreover, His design comprehended the heavens, for He gave order and perfection to the seven firmaments; and of all things He hath perfect knowledge.

Behold, thy Lord said to the angels: "I will create a vicegerent on earth." They said: "Wilt Thou place therein one who will make mischief therein and shed blood?- whilst we do celebrate Thy praises and glorify Thy holy (name)?" He said: "I know what ye know not."

And He taught Adam the nature of all things; then He placed them before the angels and said: "Tell me the nature of these if ye are right."

They said: "Glory to Thee, of knowledge We have none, save what Thou Hast taught us: In truth it is Thou Who art perfect in knowledge and wisdom."

He said: "O Adam! Tell them their natures." When he had told them, God said: "Did I not tell you that I know the secrets of heaven and earth, and I know what ye reveal and what ye conceal?"

And behold, We said to the angels: "Bow down to Adam" and they bowed down. Not so Iblis: he refused and was haughty: He was of those who reject Faith.

We said: "O Adam! dwell thou and thy wife in the Garden; and eat of the bountiful things therein as (where and when) ye will; but approach not this tree, or ye run into harm and transgression."

Then did Satan make them slip from the (garden) and get them out of the state (of felicity) in which they had been. We said: "Get ye down, all (ye people), with enmity between yourselves. On earth will be your dwelling-place and your means of livelihood - for a time."

Then learnt Adam from his Lord words of inspiration, and his Lord Turned towards him; for He is Oft-Returning, Most Merciful.

We said: "Get ye down all from here; and if, as is sure, there comes to you Guidance from me, whosoever follows My guidance, on them shall be no fear, nor shall they grieve.

"But those who reject Faith and belie Our Signs, they shall be companions of the Fire; they shall abide therein."

O Children of Israel! call to mind the (special) favor which I bestowed upon you, and fulfil your covenant with Me as I fulfil My Covenant with you, and fear none but Me.

And believe in what I reveal, confirming the revelation which is with you, and be not the first to reject Faith therein, nor sell My Signs for a small price; and fear Me, and Me alone.

And cover not Truth with falsehood, nor conceal the Truth when ye know (what it is).

And be steadfast in prayer; practice regular charity; and bow down your heads with those who bow down (in worship).

Do ye enjoin right conduct on the people, and forget (To practice it) yourselves, and yet ye study the Scripture? Will ye not understand?

Nay, seek ((God)'s) help with patient perseverance and prayer: It is indeed hard, except to those who bring a lowly spirit,-

Who bear in mind the certainty that they are to meet their

Lord, and that they are to return to Him.

Children of Israel! call to mind the (special) favor which I bestowed upon you, and that I preferred you to all other (for My Message).

Then guard yourselves against a day when one soul shall not avail another nor shall intercession be accepted for her, nor shall compensation be taken from her, nor shall anyone be helped (from outside).

And remember, We delivered you from the people of Pharaoh: They set you hard tasks and punishments, slaughtered your sons and let your women-folk live; therein was a tremendous trial from your Lord.

And remember We divided the sea for you and saved you and drowned Pharaoh's people within your very sight.

And remember We appointed forty nights for Moses, and in his absence ye took the calf (for worship), and ye did grievous wrong.

Even then We did forgive you; there was a chance for you to be grateful.

And remember We gave Moses the Scripture and the Criterion (Between right and wrong): There was a chance for you to be guided aright.

And remember Moses said to his people: "O my people! Ye have indeed wronged yourselves by your worship of the calf: So turn (in repentance) to your Maker, and slay yourselves (the wrong-doers); that will be better for you in the sight of your Maker." Then He turned towards you (in forgiveness): For He is Oft- Returning, Most Merciful.

And remember ye said: "O Moses! We shall never believe in thee until we see God manifestly," but ye were dazed with thunder and lightning even as ye looked on.

Then We raised you up after your death: Ye had the chance to be grateful.

And We gave you the shade of clouds and sent down to you Manna and quails, saying: "Eat of the good things We have provided for you:" (But they rebelled); to us they did no harm, but they harmed their own souls.

And remember We said: "Enter this town, and eat of the plenty therein as ye wish; but enter the gate with humility, in posture and in words, and We shall forgive you your faults and increase (the portion of) those who do good."

But the transgressors changed the word from that which had been given them; so We sent on the transgressors a plague from heaven, for that they infringed (Our command) repeatedly.

And remember Moses prayed for water for his people; We said: "Strike the rock with thy staff." Then gushed forth therefrom twelve springs. Each group knew its own place for water. So eat and drink of the sustenance provided by God, and do no evil nor mischief on the (face of the) earth.

And remember ye said: "O Moses! we cannot endure one kind of food (always); so beseech thy Lord for us to produce for us of what the earth groweth, -its pot-herbs, and cucumbers, Its garlic, lentils, and onions." He said: "Will ye exchange the better for the worse? Go ye down to any town, and ye shall find what ye want!" They were covered with humiliation and misery; they drew on themselves the wrath of God. This because they went on rejecting the Signs of God and slaying His Messengers without just cause. This because they rebelled and went on transgressing.

Those who believe (in the Qur'an), and those who follow the Jewish (scriptures), and the Christians and the Sabians,- any who believe in God and the Last Day, and work righteousness, shall have their reward with their Lord; on them shall be no fear, nor shall they grieve.

And remember We took your covenant and We raised above you (The towering height) of Mount (Sinai) : (Saying): "Hold firmly to what We have given you and bring (ever) to remembrance what is therein: Perchance ye may fear God."

But ye turned back thereafter: Had it not been for the Grace and Mercy of God to you, ye had surely been among the lost.

And well ye knew those amongst you who transgressed in

the matter of the Sabbath: We said to them: "Be ye apes, despised and rejected."

So We made it an example to their own time and to their posterity, and a lesson to those who fear God.

And remember Moses said to his people: "(God) commands that ye sacrifice a heifer." They said: "Makest thou a laughing-stock of us?" He said: "(God) save me from being an ignorant (fool)!"

They said: "Beseech on our behalf Thy Lord to make plain to us what (heifer) it is!" He said; "He says: The heifer should be neither too old nor too young, but of middling age. Now do what ye are commanded!"

They said: "Beseech on our behalf Thy Lord to make plain to us Her colour." He said: "He says: A fawn-coloured heifer, pure and rich in tone, the admiration of beholders!"

They said: "Beseech on our behalf Thy Lord to make plain to us what she is: To us are all heifers alike: We wish indeed for guidance, if God wills."

He said: "He says: A heifer not trained to till the soil or water the fields; sound and without blemish." They said: "Now hast thou brought the truth." Then they offered her in sacrifice, but not with good-will.

Remember ye slew a man and fell into a dispute among yourselves as to the crime: But God was to bring forth what ye did hide.

So We said: "Strike the (body) with a piece of the (heifer)." Thus God bringeth the dead to life and showeth you His Signs: Perchance ye may understand.

Thenceforth were your hearts hardened: They became like a rock and even worse in hardness. For among rocks there are some from which rivers gush forth; others there are which when split asunder send forth water; and others which sink for fear of God. And God is not unmindful of what ye do.

Can ye (o ye men of Faith) entertain the hope that they will believe in you?- Seeing that a party of them heard the Word of God, and perverted it knowingly after they understood it.

Behold! when they meet the men of Faith, they say: "We believe": But when they meet each other in private, they say: "Shall you tell them what God hath revealed to you, that they may engage you in argument about it before your Lord?"- Do ye not understand (their aim)?

Know they not that God knoweth what they conceal and what they reveal?

And there are among them illiterates, who know not the Book, but (see therein their own) desires, and they do nothing but conjecture.

Then woe to those who write the Book with their own hands, and then say: "This is from God," to traffic with it for miserable price!- Woe to them for what their hands do write, and for the gain they make thereby.

And they say: "The Fire shall not touch us but for a few numbered days:" Say: "Have ye taken a promise from God, for He never breaks His promise? or is it that ye say of God what ye do not know?"

Nay, those who seek gain in evil, and are girt round by their sins,- they are companions of the Fire: Therein shall they abide (Forever).

But those who have faith and work righteousness, they are companions of the Garden: Therein shall they abide (Forever).

And remember We took a covenant from the Children of Israel (to this effect): Worship none but God. treat with kindness your parents and kindred, and orphans and those in need; speak fair to the people; be steadfast in prayer; and practice regular charity. Then did ye turn back, except a few among you, and ye backslide (even now).

And remember We took your covenant (to this effect): Shed no blood amongst you, nor turn out your own people from your homes: and this ye solemnly ratified, and to this ye can bear witness.

After this it is ye, the same people, who slay among yourselves, and banish a party of you from their homes; assist (Their enemies) against them, in guilt and rancor; and if they come to you as captives, ye ransom them, though it was not lawful for you to banish them. Then is it only a part of the Book that ye believe in, and do ye reject the rest? but what is the reward for those among you who behave like this but disgrace in this life?- and on the Day of Judgment they shall be consigned to the most grievous penalty. For God is not unmindful of what ye do.

These are the people who buy the life of this world at the price of the Hereafter: their penalty shall not be lightened nor shall they be helped.

We gave Moses the Book and followed him up with a succession of apostles; We gave Jesus the son of Mary Clear (Signs) and strengthened him with the holy spirit. Is it that whenever there comes to you an apostle with what ye yourselves desire not, ye are puffed up with pride?- Some ye called impostors, and others ye slay!

They say, "Our hearts are the wrappings (which preserve God's Word: we need no more)." Nay, God's curse is on them for their blasphemy: Little is it they believe.

And when there comes to them a Book from God, confirming what is with them,- although from of old they had prayed for victory against those without Faith,- when there comes to them that which they (should) have recognized, they refuse to believe in it but the curse of God is on those without Faith.

Miserable is the price for which they have sold their souls, in that they deny (the revelation) which God has sent down, in insolent envy that God of His Grace should send it to any of His servants He pleases: Thus have they drawn on themselves Wrath upon Wrath. And humiliating is the punishment of those who reject Faith.

When it is said to them, "Believe in what God Hath sent down, "they say, "We believe in what was sent down to us:" yet they reject all besides, even if it be Truth confirming what is with them. Say: "Why then have ye slain the prophets of God in times gone by, if ye did indeed believe?"

There came to you Moses with clear (Signs); yet ye

worshipped the calf (Even) after that, and ye did behave wrongfully.

And remember We took your covenant and We raised above you (the towering height) of Mount (Sinai): (Saying): "Hold firmly to what We have given you, and hearken (to the Law)": They said:" We hear, and we disobey:" And they had to drink into their hearts (of the taint) of the calf because of their Faithlessness. Say: "Vile indeed are the behests of your Faith if ye have any faith!"

Say: "If the last Home, with God, be for you specially, and not for anyone else, then seek ye for death, if ye are sincere."

But they will never seek for death, on account of the (sins) which their hands have sent on before them. and God is well-acquainted with the wrong-doers.

Thou wilt indeed find them, of all people, most greedy of life,-even more than the idolaters: Each one of them wishes He could be given a life of a thousand years: But the grant of such life will not save him from (due) punishment. For God sees well all that they do.

Say: Whoever is an enemy to Gabriel-for he brings down the (revelation) to thy heart by God's will, a confirmation of what went before, and guidance and glad tidings for those who believe,-

Whoever is an enemy to God and His angels and apostles, to Gabriel and Michael,- Lo! God is an enemy to those who reject Faith.

We have sent down to thee Manifest Signs (ayat); and none reject them but those who are perverse.

Is it not (the case) that every time they make a covenant, some party among them throw it aside?- Nay, Most of them are faithless.

And when there came to them an apostle from God, confirming what was with them, a party of the people of the Book threw away the Book of God behind their backs, as if (it had been something) they did not know!

They followed what the evil ones gave out (falsely) against

the power of Solomon: the blasphemers Were, not Solomon, but the evil ones, teaching men Magic, and such things as came down at Babylon to the angels Harut and Marut. But neither of these taught anyone (Such things) without saying: "We are only for trial; so do not blaspheme." They learned from them the means to sow discord between man and wife. But they could not thus harm anyone except by God's permission. And they learned what harmed them, not what profited them. And they knew that the buyers of (magic) would have no share in the happiness of the Hereafter. And vile was the price for which they did sell their souls, if they but knew!

If they had kept their Faith and guarded themselves from evil, far better had been the reward from their Lord, if they but knew!

O ye of Faith! Say not (to the Messenger. words of ambiguous import, but words of respect; and hearken (to him): To those without Faith is a grievous punishment.

It is never the wish of those without Faith among the People of the Book, nor of the Pagans, that anything good should come down to you from your Lord. But God will choose for His special Mercy whom He will - for God is Lord of grace abounding.

None of Our revelations do We abrogate or cause to be forgotten, but We substitute something better or similar: Knowest thou not that God Hath power over all things?

Knowest thou not that to God belongeth the dominion of the heavens and the earth? And besides Him ye have neither patron nor helper.

Would ye question your Messenger as Moses was questioned of old? but whoever changeth from Faith to Unbelief, Hath strayed without doubt from the even way.

Quite a number of the People of the Book wish they could Turn you (people) back to infidelity after ye have believed, from selfish envy, after the Truth hath become Manifest unto them: But forgive and overlook, Till God accomplish His purpose; for God Hath power over all things.

And be steadfast in prayer and regular in charity: And whatever good ye send forth for your souls before you, ye shall find it with God. for God sees Well all that ye do.

And they say: "None shall enter Paradise unless he be a Jew or a Christian." Those are their (vain) desires. Say: "Produce your proof if ye are truthful."

Nay,-whoever submits His whole self to God and is a doer of good,- He will get his reward with his Lord; on such shall be no fear, nor shall they grieve.

The Jews say: "The Christians have naught (to stand) upon; and the Christians say: "The Jews have naught (To stand) upon." Yet they (Profess to) study the (same) Book. Like unto their word is what those say who know not; but God will judge between them in their quarrel on the Day of Judgment.

And who is more unjust than he who forbids that in places for the worship of God, God's name should be celebrated?- whose zeal is (in fact) to ruin them? It was not fitting that such should themselves enter them except in fear. For them there is nothing but disgrace in this world, and in the world to come, an exceeding torment.

To God belong the east and the West: Whithersoever ye turn, there is the presence of God. For God is all-Pervading, all-Knowing.

Part IV:
Indigenous Traditions

CHAPTER EIGHT

People of the Pacific

The Story of Tiddalick
(From the Australian Aborigines)

***

Somewhere in the Dreamtime…

The biggest frog in the world, Tiddalick, woke up with a great thirst. So, he drank until the land was completely dry.

Soon after, all the plants began to shrivel, and all the creatures began to turn frail.

The creatures all congregated and desperately tried to find a solution to their horrible predicament. An elderly, wise owl shared an insight: "What if Tiddalick could be made to chuckle? All the water would surely stream out of his mouth."

"How ingenious!" all the creatures exclaimed.

Once word was shared of this great insight, animals from east and west all assembled by Tiddalick's home and attempted to make him laugh. The kookaburra recounted his most entertaining tale, the kangaroo tripped over the emu and the reptile shimmied on two legs. However, no matter how hard they tried, Tiddalick remained unmoved.

Disappointment overcame them all.

With nothing else to lose, Nabunum the eel, who was driven by the draught away from his river, slid up to Tiddalick and started to dance. Nabunum began with a slow head bob, but then increased his tempo. As his dancing quickened, Nabunum began slithering around and contorted himself into various shapes.

Tiddalick seemed moved!

And after one final shape, Tiddalick exploded with laughter. Water burst freely from his mouth. And soon all parts of the land, from rivers to ponds to lakes, were once again full and flowing.

Source: original adaptation by the author.

The Rainbow Serpent: Origin of the Earth
(From the Australian Aborigines)

***

Somewhere in the Dreamtime...

The Earth was flat, and also silent, since all living things were asleep.

The Rainbow Serpent was the first to awake from beneath the earth. She was the largest, most feared creature in all of Dreamtime. With minimum effort, she pushed the ground out of her way and emerged.

The Rainbow Serpent continued her journey, traveling across the entire surface of the earth. As she moved, the ground conformed to her body. And from this, all the mountains, valleys, rivers, and lakes were made.

The Rainbow Serpent completed her journey and decided to rest. "Wake up! It is time to rise" she cried out.

The frogs were the first to emerge with bellies full of water they had stored for their hibernation. The serpent tickled them, filling up all the rivers and lakes. Trees, followed by bushes, followed by flowers, all began to grow. And soon all the birds, the reptiles, and all other animals awoke too.

The Earth was no longer flat. The Earth was also no longer silent, since all living things were now awake.

"Listen noisy ones" spoke the serpent. "I will be going to my waterhole to rest. For these gifts I have given you, I only ask that you follow my laws. For those that do, you will be made man. For those that do not, you will forever be made dirt."

From that point on, she only appeared during heavy rains when her waterhole was disturbed. From that point on, man lived among man, becoming rock when her laws were not followed.

Source: original adaptation by the author.

Tiki: The Origin of Man
(From the Maori of New Zealand)

***

Hupene, the old Tohunga, squats muttering on the floor beside his carved ancestor Tiki.

Tiki is a god who in the dim long ago helped to build the world, and whose carved image is now supporting the middle pillar of the house. His eyes of pawa-shell, which once commanded in the ten Heavens and were full of fire and wisdom, glisten out of the silent twilight; they stare far, far into the darkness, which Hine-nui-te-po is slowly spreading over the world, Hine-nui-te-po, the Great Mother of Night, who at one time was young and beautiful, and gave life to Nature.

"Haere-mai, e te manuhire, Haere-mai" ("Welcome, stranger, welcome"), so speaks the old Tohunga; then, drawing his flax mat around him, he mutters: "Haere-mai", and, after a long silence again, as if murmuring to himself, "Haere-mai"— but soon his eyes follow those of his ancestor again, gazing into the silence of the slowly descending night, the ancient goddess Hine-nui-te-po, the Great Mother of Rest. Wisdom dwells with the aged, and their muttering is the sign that their wisdom is ripe. Flying from the mouth of the old it becomes mother now and wife to the listening ear.

"Listen, my guest:

When man dies, he returns no more to the place which once knew him. Unlike the Daughter of Heaven, Te marama, the moon, which ever ascends to new life from the Spring of Living Water, man must die: he is devoured by Hine-nui-te-po, the Great Mother of Nature, the first among the gods; and man is her food.

Ha, hear now the story of Tiki, our Father, the Father of

Source: *Te Tohunga,* collected by W. Dittmer. E. P. Dutton & Co., 1907.

man!

When Rangi-nui, the great Heaven, and Papa-tu-a-nuku, the far-stretching earth, were separated from each other, then, my listener, the light shone over Papa-tu-a-nuku, the mother of Tiki, and he was the first man.

Ah, great was his longing for the power to spread himself out over Papa: father of mankind he wanted to be! Far, and far, and far he wandered over Hawaiki, searching and asking, and again and again he wandered forth over all Hawaiki, his heart full of longing.

Ah, my listener, full of longing was his heart.

At last he came to the river at Hawaiki known by the name of Wai-matu-hirangi, and from the depth of his desire he cried aloud: 'Oh, daughter of Hawaiki, child of the murmuring water, tell me how I may become the father of mankind. Tell me where may I obtain the power and from whom?'

And the river Wai-matu-hirangi answered him and said: 'Ha, Tiki, son of Heaven and Earth, go and search for the incantations and the powerful Karakias to the gods who have the desires of man in their keeping, and when you have obtained them return to me here, for it is here that the child of man shall be born: out of the murmuring waters at Hawaiki. Go, and search!'

O, listen to Tiki, our father, the father of man.

Ha!—see how he set out on his search. First he journeyed to the gods of Te Po, the Lower World, and then he made his toilsome way through the ten heavens, searching for the sacred incantations and the Karakias, the object of his mighty quest, and at last, high, high in the uppermost heaven, he found them— ah, my listener!

Joy made his journey light and the distance easy, and it was with a gladsome heart that he stood once more by the river in Hawaiki and cried aloud:

'Oh, Daughter of the Many Faces, I bring with me the Karakias to the powerful gods, the great incantations which will give power and ecstasy to Tiki. See, I bring the incantations for which I went in search.'

Then he knelt down, and, as the gods had commanded him, mixed the sacred red colour with the soft sands of the shore, and formed a figure like unto himself, as he saw his own image reflected in the water. Full of joy, he shaped the body and the limbs, the head and the eyes; and then he commenced to chant the sacred incantation, the first lines of which are as follows:

'From the children at Hawaiki,
Shake in ecstasies
Oh, shake in ecstasies
Oh, Tiki, the Father,
Tiki, the Seeker,
Ha, shake in ecstasies....'

And so, with the help of the Shimmering Heat and the Echo, the power of multiplying, he gave life to the first woman.

Marikoriko, or Twilight, was the first woman!

Marikoriko, my listener, was not a child of the gods; she was created out of the sands of the shore and the sacred Red; she takes her descent from the Shimmering Heat and from the Echo, and she became the first wife of Tiki, our father.

Many children were born to Tiki and Marikoriko his wife. Their daughter was Hine-kau-ata-ata, the Floating Shadow. And the children of Hine-kau-ata-ata began their lives as clouds, wandering across the sky. They were light and flew far away till lost to sight in the distance, or they were heavy and did not move and brooded overhead in rain. Then it was that Papa-tu-a-nuku, the Earth, lay under the spell of the first awakening day.

Among the many children of Tiki and Marikoriko were the sons the Power of Speech and the Power of Growth, who took their sisters to wife, and Te-a-io-whaka-tangata, 'He who became man', was born, and he was the father of many children—the Maori children of the world.

This is the wisdom of Tiki, our father, and Marikoriko his wife, the parents of man who peoples the earth. The wisdom of Tiki, our father.

Welcome my guest from the far distance, welcome!

You give pleasure to my eyes, and in your ears has sounded the wisdom of Tiki.—Welcome, friends of my guest.

Welcome all!

Welcome!"

has swallowed the world again and Rangi looks down upon Papa out of his Eye of Night, the moon, and is slowly unfolding his beautiful garment, which is adorned with the stars—the eyes of the braves who fell in battle.

Fiery looks Maru down upon the women who kindle the cooking-fire; Maru was the god of war in Hawaiki, but he was an evil god, full of anger and wrath, and from him are descended illness and murder. He had many enemies, and at last they killed him, and devoured him; but his spirit flew up to Rangi, there to become the fiery and flashing star.

Rauriki, the oldest among the women who kindle the cooking-fire, murmurs, for she is old, but she is a woman and murmurs no wisdom; she murmurs incantations to the fire that it might listen to Maui, who once brought the fire into the world—to be bright and warm and to cook the food for the hungry and for the guest.

Silent and peaceful is the night. The Great Mother of Nature swallows silently a few old songs and the low-toned voices that sound out of the huts and the whare-puni.

Ngawai, Rauriki's granddaughter now takes the embers to the whare-puni, and puts them to the feet of Tiki, to warm and light the house, and outside Night is working her grand and lonely wonders, while the old men, squatting around the fire and staring into the flames, narrate of the terrors of Hine-nui-te-po.

Musing and wondering thoughts light up the glow of the fire in the faces, fire flashes out of the pawa-shell eyes of the old ancestor, and patches of light flicker over the group that surrounds the fire, now lighting up the artistic lines of the tattoo in the faces, now again the phantastic carvings on the walls, or suddenly brightening a painted ornament, and covering the rest with impenetrable blackness.

Every line the light reveals, every colour it displays, gives knowledge: each carved image is a part of the history of the people. It is the family history of the group around the fire, their history painted by the god of the fire upon the black garment of night—and with the fire it will die, swallowed by Hine-nui-te-po. And so in the end all will die, the words, and the speaker, and the listener: they all will at last be devoured by Hine-nui-te-po, who has brought forth Rangi and Papa, who has brought forth Tiki, who made Marikoriko his wife.

Out of the womb of Hine-nui-te-po came the world, and to her all must go back—as the fire to the ashes.

Living in the Sky
(From the Bagobo of the Philippines)

***

Soon after people were created on the earth, there was born a child named Lumabet, who lived to be a very, very old man. He could talk when he was but one day old, and all his life he did wonderful things until the people came to believe that he had been sent by Manama, the Great Spirit.

When Lumabet was still a young man he had a fine dog, and he enjoyed nothing so much as taking him to the mountains to hunt. One day the dog noticed a white deer. Lumabet and his companions started in pursuit, but the deer was very swift and they could not catch it. On and on they went until they had gone around the world, and still the deer was ahead. One by one his companions dropped out of the chase, but Lumabet would not give up until he had the deer.

All the time he had but one banana and one camote (sweet potato) for food, but each night he planted the skins of these, and in the morning he found a banana tree with ripe fruit and a sweet potato large enough to eat. So he kept on until he had been around the world nine times, and he was an old man and his hair was gray. At last he caught the deer, and then he called all the people to a great feast, to see the animal.

While all were making merry, Lumabet told them to take a knife and kill his father. They were greatly surprised, but did as he commanded, and when the old man was dead, Lumabet waved his headband over him and he came to life again. Eight times they killed the old man at Lumabet's command, and the eighth time he was small like a little boy, for each time they had cut off some of his flesh. They all wondered very much at Lumabet's power, and they were certain that he was a god.

Source: *Philippine Folk Tales,* compiled by Mabel Cook Cole. A. C. McClurg & Co., 1916.

One morning some spirits came to talk with Lumabet, and after they had gone, he called the people to come into his house.

"We cannot all come in," said the people, "for your house is small and we are many."

"There is plenty of room," said he; so all went in and to their surprise it did not seem crowded.

Then he told the people that he was going on a long journey and that all who believed he had great power could go with him, while all who remained behind would be changed into animals and buso. He started out, many following him, and it was as he said. For those that refused to go were immediately changed into animals and buso.

He led the people far away across the ocean to a place where the earth and the sky meet. When they arrived, they saw that the sky moved up and down like a man opening and closing his jaws.

"Sky, you must go up," commanded Lumabet.

But the sky would not obey. So, the people could not go through. Finally, Lumabet promised the sky that if he would let all the others through, he might have the last man who tried to pass. Agreeing to this, the sky opened, and the people entered. But when near the last the sky shut down so suddenly that he caught not only the last man but also the long knife of the man before.

On that same day, Lumabet's son, who was hunting, did not know that his father had gone to the sky. When he was tired of the chase, he wanted to go to his father, so he leaned an arrow against a baliti tree and sat down on it. Slowly it began to go down and carried him to his father's place, but when he arrived, he could find no people. He looked here and there and could find nothing but a gun made of gold. This made him very sorrowful and he did not know what to do until some white bees which were in the house said to him:

"You must not weep, for we can take you to the sky where your father is."

So, he did as they bade, and rode on the gun, and the bees flew away with him, until in three days they reached the sky.

Now, although most of the men who followed Lumabet were content to live in the sky, there was one who was very unhappy, and all the time he kept looking down on the land below. The spirits made fun of him and wanted to take out his intestines so that he would be like them and never die, but he was afraid and always begged to be allowed to go back home.

Finally, Manama told the spirits to allow him to go, so they made a chain of the leaves of the karan grass and tied it to his legs. Then they let him down slowly head first, and when he reached the ground he was no longer a man but an owl.

The Great Flood

(From the Igorot of the Philippines)

***

Once upon a time, when the world was flat and there were no mountains, there lived two brothers, sons of Lumawig, the Great Spirit. The brothers were fond of hunting, and since no mountains had formed there was no good place to catch wild pig and deer, and the older brother said:

"Let us cause water to flow over all the world and cover it, and then mountains will rise up."

So they caused water to flow over all the earth, and when it was covered they took the head-basket of the town and set it for a trap. The brothers were very much pleased when they went to look at their trap, for they had caught not only many wild pigs and deer but also many people.

Now Lumawig looked down from his place in the sky and saw that his sons had flooded the earth and that in all the world there was just one spot which was not covered. And he saw that all the people in the world had been drowned except one brother and sister who lived in Pokis.

Then Lumawig descended, and he called to the boy and girl, saying:

"Oh, you are still alive."

"Yes," answered the boy, "we are still alive, but we are very cold."

So Lumawig commanded his dog and deer to get fire for the boy and girl. The dog and the deer swam quickly away, but though Lumawig waited a long time they did not return, and all the time the boy and girl were growing colder.

Finally, Lumawig himself went after the dog and the deer, and when he reached them he said:

Source: *Philippine Folk Tales*, compiled by Mabel Cook Cole. A. C. McClurg & Co., 1916.

"Why are you so long in bringing the fire to Pokis? Get ready and come quickly while I watch you, for the boy and girl are very cold."

Then the dog and the deer took the fire and started to swim through the flood, but when they had gone only a little way the fire was put out.

Lumawig commanded them to get more fire and they did so, but they swam only a little way again when that of the deer went out, and that of the dog would have been extinguished also had not Lumawig gone quickly to him and taken it.

As soon as Lumawig reached Pokis he built a big fire which warmed the brother and sister; and the water evaporated so that the world was as it was before, except that now there were mountains. The brother and sister married and had children, and thus there came to be many people on the earth.

CHAPTER NINE

People of the Americas

The Sacred Pipe
(From the Oglala Lakota of North America)

***

Two young men were out strolling one night talking of love affairs. They passed around a hill and came to a little ravine or coulee. Suddenly they saw coming up from the ravine a beautiful woman. She was painted and her dress was of the very finest material.

"What a beautiful girl!" said one of the young men. "Already I love her. I will steal her and make her my wife."

"No," said the other. "Don't harm her. She may be holy."

The young woman approached and held out a pipe which she first offered to the sky, then to the earth and then advanced, holding it out in her extended hands.

"I know what you young men have been saying, one of you is good; the other is wicked," she said.

She laid down the pipe on the ground and at once became a buffalo cow. The cow pawed the ground, stuck her tail straight out behind her and then lifted the pipe from the ground again in her hoofs; immediately she became a young woman again.

"I am come to give you this gift," she said. "It is the peace pipe. Hereafter all treaties and ceremonies shall be performed after smoking it. It shall bring peaceful thoughts into your minds. You shall offer it to the Great Mystery and to mother earth."

The two young men ran to the village and told what they had seen and heard. All the village came out where the young woman was. She repeated to them what she had already told the young men and added:

"When you set free the ghost (the spirit of deceased persons) you must have a white buffalo cow skin."

She gave the pipe to the medicine men of the village, turned again to a buffalo cow and fled away to the land of buffaloes.

Source: *Myths and Legends of the Sioux,* compiled by Marie L. McLaughlin, 1913.

The Deluge
(From the Cherokee of North America)

***

A long time ago a man had a dog, which began to go down to the river every day and look at the water and howl. At last the man was angry and scolded the dog, which then spoke to him and said: "Very soon there is going to be a great freshet and the water will come so high that everybody will be drowned; but if you will make a raft to get upon when the rain comes you can be saved, but you must first throw me into the water." The man did not believe it, and the dog said, "If you want a sign that I speak the truth, look at the back of my neck." He looked and saw that the dog's neck had the skin worn off so that the bones stuck out.

Then he believed the dog and began to build a raft. Soon the rain came, and he took his family, with plenty of provisions, and they all got upon it. It rained for a long time, and the water rose until the mountains were covered and all the people in the world were drowned. Then the rain stopped, and the waters went down again, until at last it was safe to come off the raft. Now there was no one alive but the man and his family, but one day they heard a sound of dancing and shouting on the other side of the ridge. The man climbed to the top and looked over; everything was still, but all along the valley he saw great piles of bones of the people who had been drowned, and then he knew that the ghosts had been dancing.

Source: *Myths of the Cherokee,* compiled by James Mooney. Government Printing Office, 1902.

The Origin of Disease & Medicine
(From the Cherokee of North America)

***

In the old days the beasts, birds, fishes, insects, and plants could all talk, and they and the people lived together in peace and friendship. But as time went on the people increased so rapidly that their settlements spread over the whole earth, and the poor animals found themselves beginning to be cramped for room. This was bad enough, but to make it worse Man invented bows, knives, blowguns, spears, and hooks, and began to slaughter the larger animals, birds, and fishes for their flesh or their skins, while the smaller creatures, such as the frogs and worms, were crushed and trodden upon without thought, out of pure carelessness or contempt. So, the animals resolved to consult upon measures for their common safety.

The Bears were the first to meet in council in their townhouse under Kuwâ'hĭ mountain, the "Mulberry place," and the old White Bear chief presided. After each in turn had complained of the way in which Man killed their friends, ate their flesh, and used their skins for his own purposes, it was decided to begin war at once against him. Someone asked what weapons Man used to destroy them. "Bows and arrows, of course," cried all the Bears in chorus. "And what are they made of?" was the next question. "The bow of wood, and the string of our entrails," replied one of the Bears. It was then proposed that they make a bow and some arrows and see if they could not use the same weapons against Man himself. So, one Bear got a nice piece of locust wood and another sacrificed himself for the good of the rest in order to furnish a piece of his entrails for the string. But when everything was ready and the first Bear stepped up to make the trial, it was found that in letting the arrow fly after

Source: *Myths of the Cherokee,* compiled by James Mooney. Government Printing Office, 1902.

drawing back the bow, his long claws caught the string and spoiled the shot. This was annoying, but someone suggested that they might trim his claws, which was accordingly done, and on a second trial it was found that the arrow went straight to the mark. But here the chief, the old White Bear, objected, saying it was necessary that they should have long claws in order to be able to climb trees. "One of us has already died to furnish the bow-string, and if we now cut off our claws, we must all starve together. It is better to trust to the teeth and claws that nature gave us, for it is plain that man's weapons were not intended for us."

No one could think of any better plan, so the old chief dismissed the council and the Bears dispersed to the woods and thickets without having concerted any way to prevent the increase of the human race. Had the result of the council been otherwise, we should now be at war with the Bears, but as it is, the hunter does not even ask the Bear's pardon when he kills one.

The Deer next held a council under their chief, the Little Deer, and after some talk decided to send rheumatism to every hunter who should kill one of them unless he took care to ask their pardon for the offense. They sent notice of their decision to the nearest settlement of Indians and told them at the same time what to do when necessity forced them to kill one of the Deer tribe. Now, whenever the hunter shoots a Deer, the Little Deer, who is swift as the wind and cannot be wounded, runs quickly up to the spot and, bending over the blood-stains, asks the spirit of the Deer if it has heard the prayer of the hunter for pardon. If the reply be "Yes," all is well, and the Little Deer goes on his way; but if the reply be "No," he follows on the trail of the hunter, guided by the drops of blood on the ground, until he arrives at his cabin in the settlement, when the Little Deer enters invisibly and strikes the hunter with rheumatism, so that he becomes at once a helpless cripple. No hunter who has regard for his health ever fails to ask pardon of the Deer for killing it, although some hunters who have not learned the prayer may try to turn aside the Little Deer from his pursuit by building a fire behind them in the trail.

Next came the Fishes and Reptiles, who had their own complaints against Man. They held their council together and determined to make their victims dream of snakes twining about them in slimy folds and blowing foul breath in their faces, or to make them dream of eating raw or decaying fish, so that they would lose appetite, sicken, and die. This is why people dream about snakes and fish.

Finally, the Birds, Insects, and smaller animals came together for the same purpose, and the Grubworm was chief of the council. It was decided that each in turn should give an opinion, and then they would vote on the question as to whether or not Man was guilty. Seven votes should be enough to condemn him. One after another denounced Man's cruelty and injustice toward the other animals and voted in favor of his death. The Frog spoke first, saying: "We must do something to check the increase of the race, or people will become so numerous that we shall be crowded from off the earth. See how they have kicked me about because I'm ugly, as they say, until my back is covered with sores;" and here he showed the spots on his skin. Next came the Bird—no one remembers now which one it was—who condemned Man "because he burns my feet off," meaning the way in which the hunter barbecues birds by impaling them on a stick set over the fire, so that their feathers and tender feet are singed off. Others followed in the same strain. The Ground-squirrel alone ventured to say a good word for Man, who seldom hurt him because he was so small, but this made the others so angry that they fell upon the Ground-squirrel and tore him with their claws, and the stripes are on his back to this day.

They began then to devise and name so many new diseases, one after another, that had not their invention at last failed them, no one of the human race would have been able to survive. The Grubworm grew constantly more pleased as the name of each disease was called off, until at last they reached the end of the list, when someone proposed to make menstruation sometimes fatal to women. On this he rose up in his place and cried:

"*Wadâñ'!* [Thanks!] I'm glad some more of them will die, for they are getting so thick that they tread on me." The thought fairly made him shake with joy, so that he fell over backward and could not get on his feet again, but had to wriggle off on his back, as the Grubworm has done ever since.

When the Plants, who were friendly to Man, heard what had been done by the animals, they determined to defeat the latters' evil designs. Each Tree, Shrub, and Herb, down even to the Grasses and Mosses, agreed to furnish a cure for some one of the diseases named, and each said: "I shall appear to help Man when he calls upon me in his need." Thus came medicine; and the plants, every one of which has its use if we only knew it, furnish the remedy to counteract the evil wrought by the revengeful animals. Even weeds were made for some good purpose, which we must find out for ourselves. When the doctor does not know what medicine to use for a sick man the spirit of the plant tells him.

The Creation of All Things
(From the Aztecs of Mexico)

***

At a certain time four brothers gathered together and consulted concerning the creation of things. The work was left to Quetzalcoatl and Huitzilopochtli. First they made fire, then half a sun, the heavens, the waters and a certain great fish therein, called Cipactli, and from its flesh the solid earth. The first mortals were the man, Cipactonal, and the woman, Oxomuco, and that the son born to them might have a wife, the four gods made one for him out of a hair taken from the head of their divine mother, Xochiquetzal.

Now began the struggle between the two brothers, Tezcatlipoca and Quetzalcoatl, which was destined to destroy time after time the world, with all its inhabitants, and to plunge even the heavenly luminaries into a common ruin.

The half sun created by Quetzalcoatl lighted the world but poorly, and the four gods came together to consult about adding another half to it. Not waiting for their decision, Tezcatlipoca transformed himself into a sun, whereupon the other gods filled the world with great giants, who could tear up trees with their hands. When an epoch of thirteen times fifty-two years had passed, Quetzalcoatl seized a great stick, and with a blow of it knocked Tezcatlipoca from the sky into the waters, and himself became sun. The fallen god transformed himself into a tiger and emerged from the waves to attack and devour the giants with which his brothers had enviously filled the world which he had been lighting from the sky. After this, he passed to the nocturnal heavens, and became the constellation of the Great Bear.

For an epoch the earth flourished under Quetzalcoatl as sun, but Tezcatlipoca was merely biding his time, and the epoch ended, he appeared as a tiger and gave Quetzalcoatl such a blow with his paw that it hurled him from the skies. The overthrown

---

Source: *American Hero-Myths*, compiled by Daniel G. Brinton, 1882.

god revenged himself by sweeping the earth with so violent a tornado that it destroyed all the inhabitants but a few, and these were changed into monkeys. His victorious brother then placed in the heavens, as sun, Tlaloc, the god of darkness, water and rains, but after half an epoch, Quetzalcoatl poured a flood of fire upon the earth, drove Tlaloc from the sky, and placed in his stead, as sun, the goddess Chalchiutlicue, the Emerald Skirted, wife of Tlaloc. In her time the rains poured so upon the earth that all human beings were drowned or changed into fishes, and at last the heavens themselves fell, and sun and stars were alike quenched.

Then the two brothers whose strife had brought this ruin, united their efforts and raised again the sky, resting it on two mighty trees, the Tree of the Mirror (*tezcaquahuitl*) and the Beautiful Great Rose Tree (*quetzalveixochitl*), on which the concave heavens have ever since securely rested; though we know them better, perhaps, if we drop the metaphor and call them the "mirroring sea" and the "flowery earth," on one of which reposes the horizon, in whichever direction we may look.

Again the four brothers met together to provide a sun for the now darkened earth. They decided to make one, indeed, but such a one as would eat the hearts and drink the blood of victims, and there must be wars upon the earth, that these victims could be obtained for the sacrifice. Then Quetzalcoatl built a great fire and took his son--his son born of his own flesh, without the aid of woman--and cast him into the flames, whence he rose into the sky as the sun which lights the world. When the Light-God kindles the flames of the dawn in the orient sky, shortly the sun emerges from below the horizon and ascends the heavens. Tlaloc, god of waters, followed, and into the glowing ashes of the pyre threw his son, who rose as the moon.

Tezcatlipoca had it now in mind to people the earth, and he, therefore, smote a certain rock with a stick, and from it issued four hundred barbarians (*chichimeca*). Certain five goddesses, however, whom he had already created in the eighth heaven, descended and slew these four hundred, all but three. These goddesses likewise died before the sun appeared, but came into being again from the garments they had left behind. So also did the four hundred Chichimecs, and these set about to burn one of the five goddesses, by name Coatlicue, the Serpent Skirted, because it was discovered that she was with child, though yet unmarried. But, in fact, she was a spotless virgin, and had known no man. She had placed some white plumes in her bosom, and through these the god Huitzilopochtli entered her body to be born again. When, therefore, the four hundred had gathered together to burn her, the god came forth fully armed and slew them everyone.

The Making of Man & Maize

(From the Iroquois of North America)

***

The earth was covered with water, in which dwelt aquatic animals and monsters of the deep. Far above it were the heavens, peopled by supernatural beings. One day, Ataensic, threw herself through a rift in the sky and fell toward the earth. She fell from heaven down to the primeval waters. There a turtle offered her his broad back as a resting-place until, from a little mud which was brought her, either by a frog, a beaver or some other animal, she, by magic power, formed dry land on which to reside.

At the time she fell from the sky she was pregnant, and in due time was delivered of a daughter. This daughter grew to womanhood and conceived without having seen a man, for none was as yet created. The product of her womb was twins, and even before birth one of them betrayed his restless and evil nature, by refusing to be born in the usual manner, but insisting on breaking through his parent's side (or armpit). He did so, but it cost his mother her life. Her body was buried, and from it sprang the various vegetable productions which the new earth required to fit it for the habitation of man. From her head grew the pumpkin vine; from her breast, the maize; from her limbs, the bean and other useful esculents.

Meanwhile the two brothers grew up. The one was named Ioskeha. He went about the earth, which at that time was arid and waterless, and called forth the springs and lakes, and formed the sparkling brooks and broad rivers. But his brother, the troublesome Tawiscara, he whose obstinacy had caused their mother's death, created an immense frog which swallowed all the water and left the earth as dry as before. Ioskeha was informed of this by the partridge, and immediately set out for his brother's country, for they had divided the earth between them.

Source: *American Hero-Myths*, compiled by Daniel G. Brinton, 1882.

Soon he came to the gigantic frog and piercing it in the side (or armpit), the waters flowed out once more in their accustomed ways. Then it was revealed to Ioskeha by his mother's spirit that Tawiscara intended to slay him by treachery. Therefore, when the brothers met, as they soon did, it was evident that a mortal combat was to begin.

Now, they were not men, but gods, whom it was impossible really to kill, nor even could either be seemingly slain, except by one particular substance, a secret which each had in his own keeping. As therefore a contest with ordinary weapons would have been vain and unavailing, they agreed to tell each other what to each was the fatal implement of war. Ioskeha acknowledged that to him a bag filled with maize was more dangerous than anything else; and Tawiscara disclosed that the horn of a deer could alone reach his vital part.

They laid off the lists, and Tawiscara, having the first chance, attacked his brother violently with a bag filled with maize, and beat him till he lay as one dead; but quickly reviving, Ioskeha assaulted Tawiscara with the antler of a deer, and dealing him a blow in the side, the blood flowed from the wound in streams. The unlucky combatant fled from the field, hastening toward the west, and as he ran the drops of his blood which fell upon the earth turned into flint stones. Ioskeha did not spare him, but hastening after, finally slew him. He did not, however, actually kill him, for, as I have said, these were beings who could not die; and, in fact, Tawiscara was merely driven from the earth and forced to reside in the far west, where he became ruler of the spirits of the dead. These go there to dwell when they leave the bodies behind them here.

Ioskeha, returning, peaceably devoted himself to peopling the land. He opened a cave which existed in the earth and allowed to come forth from it all the varieties of animals with which the woods and prairies are peopled. In order that they might be more easily caught by men, he wounded everyone in the foot except the wolf, which dodged his blow; for that reason, this beast is one of the most difficult to catch. He then formed men and gave them life, and instructed them in the art of making fire, which he himself had learned from the great tortoise. Furthermore, he taught them how to raise maize, and it is, in fact, Ioskeha himself who imparts fertility to the soil, and through his bounty and kindness the grain returns a hundred-fold.

The Beginning of Light & Death

(From the Eskimos of the Arctic)

***

Our forefathers have told us much of the coming of earth, and of men, and it was a long, long while ago. Those who lived long before our day, they did not know how to store their words in little black marks, as you do; they could only tell stories. And they told of many things, and therefore we are not without knowledge of these things, which we have heard told many and many a time, since we were little children. Old women do not waste their words idly, and we believe what they say. Old age does not lie.

A long, long time ago, when the earth was to be made, it fell down from the sky. Earth, hills and stones, all fell down from the sky, and thus the earth was made.

And then, when the earth was made, came men.

It is said that they came forth out of the earth. Little children came out of the earth. They came forth from among the willow bushes, all covered with willow leaves. And there they lay among the little bushes: lay and kicked, for they could not even crawl. And they got their food from the earth.

Then there is something about a man and a woman, but what of them? It is not clearly known. When did they find each other, and when had they grown up? I do not know. But the woman sewed, and made children's clothes, and wandered forth. And she found little children, and dressed them in the clothes, and brought them home.

And in this way men grew to be many.

And being now so many, they desired to have dogs. So, a man went out with a dog leash in his hand, and began to stamp on the ground, crying "Hok—hok—hok!" Then the dogs came

---

Source: *Eskimo Folk-Tales*, compiled by Knud Rasmussen and translated by W. Worster. Glydendal, 1921.

hurrying out from the hummocks, and shook themselves violently, for their coats were full of sand. Thus men found dogs.

But then children began to be born, and men grew to be very many on the earth. They knew nothing of death in those days, a long, long time ago, and grew to be very old. At last they could not walk, but went blind, and could not lie down.

Neither did they know the sun, but lived in the dark. No day ever dawned. Only inside their houses was there ever light, and they burned water in their lamps, for in those days water would burn.

But these men who did not know how to die, they grew to be too many, and crowded the earth. And then there came a mighty flood from the sea. Many were drowned, and men grew fewer. We can still see marks of that great flood, on the high hill-tops, where mussel shells may often be found.

And now that men had begun to be fewer, two old women began to speak thus:

"Better to be without day, if thus we may be without death," said the one.

"No; let us have both light and death," said the other.

And when the old woman had spoken these words, it was as she had wished. Light came, and death.

It is said, that when the first man died, others covered up the body with stones. But the body came back again, not knowing rightly how to die. It stuck out its head from the bench and tried to get up. But an old woman thrust it back, and said:

"We have much to carry, and our sledges are small."

For they were about to set out on a hunting journey. And so the dead one was forced to go back to the mound of stones.

And now, after men had got light on their earth, they were able to go on journeys, and to hunt, and no longer needed to eat of the earth. And with death came also the sun, moon and stars.

For when men die, they go up into the sky and become brightly shining things there.

Other Works by the Author

Venturing into Philosophy
Authentic Happiness in Seven Emails
The Power of Thinking Differently

www.ingramcontent.com/pod-product-compliance
Lightning Source LLC
Chambersburg PA
CBHW031546040426
42452CB00006B/211